Charles Godfrey Leland

Hans Breitmann in Germany

Tyrol

Charles Godfrey Leland

Hans Breitmann in Germany
Tyrol

ISBN/EAN: 9783743311893

Manufactured in Europe, USA, Canada, Australia, Japa

Cover: Foto ©ninafisch / pixelio.de

Manufactured and distributed by brebook publishing software (www.brebook.com)

Charles Godfrey Leland

Hans Breitmann in Germany

IN MEMORY OF MANY A KIND WORD FITLY SPOKEN, THIS WORK IS GRATEFULLY DEDICATED BY THE AUTHOR TO

GEORGE A. SALA.

Dus shpoke der Meister Trongemond,
Who two und sefenty Lands had knowned;
"*Fremde Sitten, fremdes Land*
Macht dich mit Dir selbst bekannt;"
"Foreign Life und Lands I trow,
Make a Man himself to know,
But at Home, ash on a Shelf,
You'll nefer learn to know Yourself."

Troo de forests, troo de valleys,
Like a leaf py preezes hurled,
From de palace to de galleys,
Ve pehold a various worldt.
Id is bleasant ven we wander,
Troo such shiften scenes, indeed,
Und likevise ven we can ponder,
Ofer vot in pooks we read:
For you meet mit many sages,
See fool many tafern-signs,
Dravellin' ofer brinted pages,
On de pat'way of de lines.
'Tis not always yoost py shpeedin'
Troo a land dot we crow wise;
Many a man has learnt py readin'
More dan vot he saw mit eyes:
Men who troo de vorldt hafe scudded,
Of exberience make a poast,
Boot we find dot dose who've studied,
Is de vons vot see de most;
He dot's learned in Art und History,

He vot *dinks* while yet at home—
Is de Mann dot find no mysdery
In de *Länder* vhere he roam ;
He vot's learnet to sing de pallads
Efen from pooks—vote'er pefal—
Talk de language—mix de salads,—
Dakes de shine out of dem all !
Dus de buzzle is onravelled,
Dough id may seem sdrange to some,
Dat de men who moost hafe trafelled,
Ofden nefer left deir home ;
Reading vakens expecdadion ;
Expecdadion preeds tesire ;
Ach! *wie schön* die gonsummation
Ven we kit vot we require !
Derefore BREITMANN, who, like 'Lysses,
Hafe seen men und cities too,
Known Life's heighds mit ids apysses,
Scribed dis liddle pook fer you,
Hopin' dot his Drafel-Bictures,
Dough not plessed mit too moosh learnin',
Und too liaple to strigtures,
Shdill may vake in you de yearnin'
To pehold de tifferent beoples,
Lands mit castles, downs mit towers ;
Dom-catedrals mit deir shdeebles ;
Kinder—Mädchen—Gartens—vlowers—
Und die *Almen* on de Alpen
In de *Sonne* like *Smaragd*,

Und de roads mit *Reiters* gall'pen
On deir horses to de *Jagd*,
Und de dorrents doun de rockses,
In der *schöne* land Tyrol;
Und die *Senn'rin* tendin' flockses
In her *schwarze Kamisol*.
Und de Kneips of de *Studenten*,
Vhere you paws to squinch your durst—
Garküche mit Hühnchen—Enten—
Sauer-kraut und Leber-Wurst,
Dices rattlin—vellers jokin'
Mit de beer-maids *schmuck* and tall;
Glasses foamin—Burschen shmokin,
Wreaths a hangin' on de wall,
Ach die bunten schönen Bilder,
Dot pefore mein fision bass!
Vot enrapdure und pewilder,
Yoost like bictures in a glass,
Dot coom peepin' sdrangely at you,
Shdartlin' at you ven you least expec';
Like de *Muttergottes* sdatue
From deir *Nische* on de *Eck'*.
Oh dot all my Memory musters,
Yoost might bass indo my ben,
Und like grapes in shinin' clusters
Send goot wein to you again!
For de pizness of de writer
Ist not merely to repeat,
Boot to make his sgetch, dough lighter,

5

Mit a sbirit shdill more sweet :—
Nun !—der Breitmann may hafe missed it :
Dough he roamed from Ost to West,
Boot howefer fate may twist it,
Shdill he did his lefel best :
Tid his pest in hopeful shpirit ;
Dot's mit hope to bleasure *you :*
Vorkin hardt some braise to merid—
More dan dot no man can do.

CONTENTS.

	PAGE
PRELIMINARY NOTICE	11

CHAP.
I. ON SHILDREN'S PLAYS, MIT DER BALLADE OF
HIES'L DER PAD LIDDLE POY . . 25
II. ON DE GIGANTIC VIRDUE OF GERMAN PATIENCE,
MIT DE HISTORIE OF GERMAN GIANTS IN
TIROL 35
III. ON DE HAPIT OF SHTARIN' AT STRANGERS—
DENN ON TREATIN' PEOPLE AS FOOLS
UND ITS CRATE DANGER. DE BALLADE
OF NARR-HANS'L 51
IV. WHY DE GERMAN TOURISTS DO TELESCOPES
CARRY. DE YANKEE GALS MIT A SPY-
GLASS UND VOT DEY SAW! DE BALLAD
OF KATRINA BAUER WHO DE PROFESSOR
KILLED 65
V. OF DE TOUN OF HALL, WITCH IS ALL PE-SALTED.
HOW DER BREITMANN THIRSDY GOT, UND
MADE LOFE TO DE PEAUDIFUL BEER
GIRL. DE SHTORY OF GEORG'L, UND DE
WONDERFUL BALLADE OF DER GOAT MIT
DER SHPOON 75

Contents.

CHAP.		PAGE
VI.	VY DE ALL-ALONELINESS OF NATUR MIT SPOOKS AND OFER-NATURAL PEIN'S GEFILLED IS. DE BALLAD-SHTORIES OF DE KAUNSER-WITCH—DE HAZEL-WITCH—DIE BELL OF KALTEIN UND DIE WOONDERFULL PEASE	105
VII.	A SHTORY FROM BOTZEN—DE DEAD HEAD VOT MAKE DE FORTUNE OF DER STUDENT JOHANNES	133
VIII.	ON TYROLESE FIG-COFFEE UND DE SOCIOLOGICAL DEDUCTIONS FROM IT. MIT A BALLADE APOUT DIS DING OF CHEMICAL META-GENESES UND MYSDERIÖS METASTASES	145

TYROL.

DE TYROL.

EINLEITUNG ÜND VORSTELLUNG, OR DER INTRODUCTION.

As dere is no gettin' into an friendtship mitout acquaindance—und no way to kit broperly into Acquaintance mitout an Introduction, I dink it would pe fery peautiful to make a liddle von for de Tyrol, yoost here, in de apropopriate blace; or in de Begin; fer ash de proferb say, *Die rechte Zeit und die schlecte Zeit, mein Lieber—beide gehn vorüber:*

> Right dimes, or wrong or pad dey say
> Moost mit der Time all bass afay.

Now dis vouldt pe de right dime und blace, cerdainly, to mendion all de books dot efer was scribed on de Tyrol,—since dot shows vot a donderin lot de learnet author hafe readt,—

Preliminary Notice.

und so I a *poema* pegun, mit de ditles of all de Buchs dot efer were maket on dis sobyect—vot in dis wise goed :

Oh den, oh Muse vot fire de poet's soul,
Yoost help me mit de Buchs on de Tyrol!
Dere's foorst of all in Englisch und in German:
"Through the Aaltberg" by Ludewig von Hörmann—
Und denn Herr Grohmann mit an artisdt's ease,
Wrote "Die Tyrol-land, and de Tyrolese."
" De Hol'days in Tyrol " py Walter White
Was also gife de readers moosh telight,
"Untrotten Beaks und Oonfrequented Valleys"
Vas von of 'Melia Edwards' prilliant sallies
(I knew dot laity, und I hafe gonfest
Dot she vas learned 'mong de learnedest) ;
"De Valleys of Tirol," py Miss R. Busk,
Ist like a fairy-legend read at dusk ;
(Dis writeress too I met von dimes in Rome).
Amththor's *Tirolerführer* is a plum,
De *Illustrirter Führer* durch de Alps,
Among de Buchs mit bictures dake de scalps ;
De "Gossensass," by Noe, is a dreat
(Roast Goose mit Appel-sass ist alfays shweet).
Mit Goosensass likewise to pass your time,
Dere is "Roswitha," named "Von Gandersheim,"[1]

---

[1] "Roswitha von Gandersheim," 80 pfennig. Universal-Bibliothek, von P. Reclam, Leipzig, 1894.

Preliminary Notice.

Pecause vot Natur' yoins we should not sunder,
Sauce for de Goose is also for de Gander;
"Auf Etsch und Eisach," by Brachvogel too—
(*Brach*vogel means a plover, dot is true—
In life, ash at de table, 'tis de use
To see de "game" a-followin' de goose.)
Drei Sommer in Tirol, py Ludwig Steub,
May enderdain you ash you shmokes your pipe.
Berg, Burg und Thalfarten bei M'ran und Bozen,
Maket men take Alpenstocks und pull deir coats on!
Und mit telight to set you all a-cryin',
Dere's Ignaz Zingerle his *Schildereien :*
Also a liddle *Buch,* py C. H. C.
On Innsbruck gifen to guests, py Charles Landsee,
Vot keept de foorst hotel in all de blace:
A work, dough small, reblete mit sense und grace.
Good—like de nople house from vitch it cooms :—
In dot *Tiroler Hof* I hafe mine rooms,
Und from its name it flashed indo my soul,
To write dis work oopon das Land Tyrol—

But when he hat cot dus far——de aut'or is beshamed to say dot he shtop short und proke toun oonder de hoomiliadin' reflecdion——dot mit de excepdion of de last-mendionet he hafe not seen de first von of all dese books—und really know nodings at all apout dem—teufel a pit! Now I bote veel und know dot efery veteran

Preliminary Notice.

of de press (yea, und efen de fery girl-peginners), moost tespise soosh a *krankhafte Gewissenhaftigkeit*, or morpid conscientiousness, in a man vot hafing de whole List of Buchs pefore him, maket any scruple of rottlin' on apout dem as if he hat de whole py hearts, *Lock und Stock*—*ganz und gar*. *Nun, gut*, dere is no help for id ——id isn't in me. So I givet id oop!

Denn a *frische Idee* let idself in oopon my Mind, ash an old proferb rosed oop like a shtar into de ooter leaden mitnight of my *bedunkelte Seele*,—und dot vas:

"Welcher Esel die Pauken nicht kann schlagen,
Muss die Säck' zur Mühle tragen."

[A donkey vot gannot peat on a drum,
Still may garry de sacks from de mill to home.]

Und id gome to me as a *ganz origineller Gedanke*, or notion vot nopody efer hat pefore, inshtet of makin' mein work oud of oder *Buchs*—to write id endirely out of mine own het, und exberiences—und nod *porrow* nodings from Nopody—of any gonsequence. To pe sure dis is roonin'

Preliminary Notice.

crate risks, for, ash efery pooplisher knows, Novelties in Literatur are fery tangerous—und dis is von of de most shtartin kind. Howefer, dot is de way it was done. Now de Werlt is cot to pe so wicked, und de dricks of de Trade is pecome so numperless, dot dere will pe Volks who will occuse me of hoompuggin, efen here—yoost ash der Teufel said to de holy Hermit, "Thou art a sanctimonious hypocritic" (as is told py Agricola)—boot if any soosh dere are, dey may yoost shear off to dem teufel und shake demselfs.

Denn acain, I have tone—vot indeed no German writer *efer* tid pefore me, since de fery peginning of dime, or de fore-gone Edernity—und avoidet afery tempdation to display mine learnin' or form theories of Origins of names in Hishtorie. Dus, for example, when I foundt out dot Nopody really knew pefore me vot de wort Tyrol means—und de undeniaple truth coom to me ash I learnt id from an old peasant-*Bauer*—I shdill refrainet from mentionin' id. For id abbears dot de early inhopitants of dis landt who were *Giants*, lifed on dop of de moundains, und ven dey wanted to go into Innsbruck, dey

Preliminary Notice.

yoost *rolled* doun into de valley, from whence dey were callet *De Rollers*, or Ty-rolers—albeit I was tolt py a Suabian *Gelehrter*, or learnet man, dot it was more likely dot it come from *rollbar*, or *de rollin'* of de tongue, pecause de unhappytants of dis favoured land are so giftet mit gab, und hafe *proverpially* so much *Schwatzhaftigkeit* or loquacity.

I hafe also refrain from mentionin' dot *Innsbruck* commed from de Wort *In* und *Bruch*, a bog or flat blace or site, und nod from de rifer *Inn* and *Brücke*, a pridge, vitch latter is indeet fery plausiple, und naturly hafe misleated many shmall soaperficial foolologists. Somedings may howefer be said for de Théorie dot id is derivet from de *Inns* or hotels vitch hafe pecome so common since de Englisch volk hafe dook to comin' here, vitch *schiessen wie die Pilze aus der Bruch' hervor*—dot is vitch shoot like mushrooms from der *Bruch'* or level ground—py which it is also interestin' to be-mark dot *mushrooms* intimate dot dere is so mush, or much, or so many rooms in dem.

All dese demptations hafe I most oonscrupu-

Preliminary Notice.

lusly avoidet to show de Reater dot it is bossiple, efen for a German writer on Deutsche soobyects in a German land, to geep glear of all Germanism ven he redress a British American *publicum*, hafin' mineself, like dem, a crate *Abscheu* or horrorple disgoost for too much talkativeness—alvays pearin in mind de wise sayin' of Walter von der Vogelweide, who vas himself a Tyroler :

> " Keep a guardt oopon your tongue,
> Dat is goot for oldt or young ;
> Shut de polt pefore de door,
> Speak no idle wort no more." [1]

Now dere is anoder fery crate Originality in dis Buch. As it has peen saidt, " few men can live mitout a master or a wife," so dere is no German dot can write oonless under de over-rulin' needcessity, und iron rule of de Unities, or makin his whole Buch a logical und gon-

> [1] Hütet iuwer zungen,
> Das zîmt wol den jungen ;
> Stoz den rigel vür die tür,
> La de keine boese wort dafür.

Preliminary Notice.

nectet whole ; vereas dis of mine gonsists altogeter of *Skizzen,* or Skits, or Skitches of dings, yoost ash dey comed along. Dere is a curious oldt proverb dat " ven der Rhein is vonce in de Ocean he nefer dinks of the Ill " —dot is a liddle rill vot roon into id. Yoost so, most trafel-writers try to pe Seas or keep de sea in sight—vhile dis mein Buch is all of rivulets !

> So oop and down, denn roonin' pack,
> Like waves on de beach at play ;
> Und fitful ash a yoompin Yack,
> Our fancies flit afay.

Und so id is, oh reater—dot de mind of de Drafeller, drawn from object to object, yoomps from idée to idée like a monkey from pranch to pranch in a dropical forest—for vitch reason I hafe made dis chapder motley und varied, dat you may oonderstand from de peginnin', or *Anfang* (so callet pecause it is dere dot men catch holt), dot dis Buch vill pe a changin' kaleidoscope, und not a panorama of von subject —a work multiform und multifarious, of characder manifold und *vielseitig,* or many-sided, yea,

Preliminary Notice.

heteregeneous, motley, mosaic, indiskcriminal, desultory (und Liberal), irreckular und reckless, diverse und prose, all sorts of kinds und unkinds, *et hoc genus omne und vot nod?—de omnibus rebus et quibusdam aliis.*

For de man who drafels most is de von who sees de most—und dinks de most in cratest Variety—und nod de von who yoost cofer de most groundt. Derefore, ash you will fore-saw, dere will pe a crate deal of fery fine confused feedin' in dis Buch.

(*A bause.*)

. . . *Doch weiter*—mine tear reader—yoost, a liddle few words more!

It comed to pass oopon a dimes vonce dat a crate gramme-arian—or von of de kindt dat himself mit liddle grains or pig scruples efer busies in language, to me told, dot he didn't dink moosh of mine Teutonic English, pecause I de same worts *sehr oft* fery decidedly und tifferently bronounced und written hafe. Vitch ist fery drue, und I mineself dereto spécial attention do call. For I peg you all to be-

Preliminary Notice.

mark dat dere was yet nefer porn nor on dis Eart' a humane bein'—und most of all a Deutscher immortal—who while learnin' a language—I gare not vot or vhen—tid not somedimes bronounce or out-speak in two or dree tifferent ways de same ding. I dink dis learned Mann "*hat mir eigentlich nicht in die Pfanne gehaut,*" or "not got de petter in a controfersy" ash der Herr BORCHARDT exblain de sayin', vitch mean literally, to coot anypody up to liddle bieces, und denn *fry 'em!* Now —not to talk too moosh—I mendion all dis to remint der Reader dat de diversification und dissim-hilarity mismatchedness of de shpellin' is de result of crate und profound study of mine vellow-countrymen vot hafe nod as yet ottain to soosh broficiency in English as Mineself. Now I shvear, py mine Ink und Penstand! dot it ist no half hour since I dalk English mit a Tyroler, und may I pe plessed if dot veller bronouncet any dwo Worts alike—*sogar auf Deutsch,* he saidt, "*Jao-ja*" for "Yes, yes." One wouldt dink dot his expressions all saidt of von anoder vot der Teufel saidt of de

Preliminary Notice.

chimney-shweep : "*Lass ihn ein—er ist mir ähnlich*"—"Let him com' in—he looks someding like me."

Und yet furder : It ofden happen dot de Critikers or Crickets, efen vhen dey are ooterly or oonooteraply telightet mit a Buch, all de way troo, shtill vant to find some *liddle Fehlers* or faults, so ash to abbear imbartial. Und to shpare dem disples I hafe here und dere put in some bloonders und defects, to oplige dem. Und aldough it is saidt *Aquila non captat muscas* (Eacles tont hawk at vlies), shtill dere is som' who cotch at brinter's errors, *et cetera*, und hint dem all on de author—aldough he may hafe corrected dem tree dimes ofer—as has ofden happened to me, mineself ; now, to oplige dem, I hafe gemaket seferal dings all wrong—yoost to help 'em along—may der Lort brosper oos all in our kindly intentions ! So dot if de reader find anyding dot tid not gefall or blease him, I peg him to rememper dot it vas poot in *mit Absicht* or fell intention, to prefent *das Buch* from pein' *too* goot. Wouldt dot all writers hat dis *Bescheidenheit*

Preliminary Notice.

or Modesty, like me, und nod make demselfs oppear as *schamlos* py pretendin' to perfecdion!

It is dis veelin' of irrebressiple modesty vot me dus far prefented hafe from mention vot a crate-full-ologist to me oncet expressed at an Oriental Congresse—und it vas priefly dis: "Vhen de vlyin machine of Maxim shall hafe pecome an Axiom or estaplished Sayin' or Trut'—und avery pody vly efery where—like pumple-pees—denn de oferpowerin' preponterance of de English or Angelic-Saxon und German races vill it to pass pring dot *Breitmannese* vill pe de sole language of de future for de entire human races! Dot is to say dot Pidgin English mit German gemixt, und mitout any bodders of grammar or shbellin', or syntaxes, or any oder kinds of taxes on our sins or impatiences, will bredominate—und dere you are!" "*Dot'll* set 'em up a dalkin" —ash de old lady said ven she put rum in her visidors' tea—"if anyding will"—und it tid! I leafe de gontemblation of dis stubendous future to my reaters!

Also it was beknown dot de studie of de

Preliminary Notice.

Breitmann writings form de pest und casiest *Einleitung*, dot is an In-leading or Introduction to de German language dot is as yet refealed to humanity, or de *Menschheit*. I go not far as a friendt of mein in Philadelphia tid, vot teclare dot readin' dem made him veel more Dutchy as de Dutches demselfs—*Germanior quam Germanos ipsos*—for I feer dot was mere fluttery. Dere is, however, von liddle anecdòte which I myself to omit not can pring. In a high, well-born Englisch *Familie*, where de German unto de shildren ge-learned was, dese yung uns access had to a copie of mine Ballads, which dey py hearts got. Und de result was dot dey beginned to talk to von anoder in soosh a Dialekte dot *die Mutter* de first wort of vot dey saidt not understand could—*sogar* a North German dot dere came, teclared he only a liddle here and dere begripped. Boot ven in dot familie a Professor from Tübingen arrifed—he listen like von who was ruptured mit telight, und denn to de Mutter said: "Madame, I hafe in de most cultured circles in England peen, boot anyding so understand-

Preliminary Notice.

aple as de speechfullness of your shildren, I nefer ge-heard hafe." Und ven dese kinders to Munich ge-taken were, de fery foorst tay dey shut up de cook mit sass, und shkared a *Schornsteinfeger*, or chimply-shweep, *white!* I att no more!

Doch!—yet von more remark. Der Tübinger Professor, of whom I spoken hafe, ven he left England, put on his cards, B.B.C., dot is *Bour Brendre Congé*—so I adds hier a Bébé S—or a post-postscript — dot is dot if de public like dis Buch apout de Tirol, dere may vollow bossiply Hans Breitmann in Italy—or New Jersey—or Brighton—or Egypt—or Russland—or in Zigeunerland, vitch is Eferywhere—yoost as de Sales, und de Critics may determine —I peing guidet brincipally py de first und mostly py de last. Und dis is, I peliefe, mine last Wort. Now you may pegin readin de Buch!

CHAPTER I.

ON SHILDREN'S PLAYS, MIT DER BALLADE OF HIES'L DER PAD LIDDLE POY.

"Daz was noch gar ein Kindes spil."
WOLFRAM VON ESCHENBACH, *Parzival* (557, 12).

"Cavalcar la capra verso il chino."
Proverbii di Orlando Peschetti, 1618.

DER BREITMANN sat in a gorner of de peaudiful public Garden, or Park, of Innsbruck—or in dat spezial *Ecke* vhere de pest Lager Bier is dispenset py de Geschwister Tiefenthaler under de shady drees—*alles sehr schön*—und he vatch a ten or dwelf liddle girls, von of vitch vas a shmall poy in an old-vashioned coat doun to his heels like a Noah's Ark, und a long cock-tails in his hat.

Dey were a-blayin a *Kindspiel* a game, vitch

Hans Breitmann in

dey egsecutit dusly : Dey all make a ring und danced roundt, a-singin' in Deutsch—

> "Im Frühling, im Frühling
> Da ist die schönste Zeit,
> Da freuen sich die Junge
> Und auch die Alte heut,"

> [De Spring-dime—de Spring-dime,
> Dot is de fairest, true,
> Denn young folk all rejoices,
> Likevise de old vons too.]

Den de shildren shtopped and sang—

> "Der Schuster, der Schuster,
> Der macht es immer so."

> [Der shoemak'er, der shoemak'er,
> He always work yoost so !]

Den de Kinders all pegan to make pelieve bore holes mit awls in de Ledder and make schuhs. Denn dey all *tantz* round again and sing—

> "In Spring-time, in Spring-time,"

und denn dey imitated a *Schulmeister*, ven all

de pig shildren vip de shmall vons, and der liddle poy cot pehind-shpanked vorst of all, dough he hat peen der most shtillest and pestest in de whole gommunity. Denn dey goed on to show how deir Vater shmoked a pipe, und die house-maid shweep de vloor, und der Onkel trink bier, und so on mit all de oder Industriell bursuits und avocadions of de mittel class—mit de Tantz-chorus.

"Dot blay," remark der Herr Professor Bumbelchen, vot had accompanit Hans to dis Szene of innocent Mirt' und jufenile *Festivität*—" is drawn from de Mittel Ages, vot dook it in toorn from de more older dimes of Rome—und id was an apridged form of de vamous *Gewerbszüge*, a processions of de trades, in which dey march singin' de praises of Spring, while dey practise deir callings."

"*Ja, so!*" rebly Hans. "*Das ist aber sehr interessant.* Dot is fery inderestin'."

"De shildrens," pursued der Herr Professor, " are de chroniclers und breserfers of more folk-lore, dann de Worlt dinks of."

"I hafe observet," remarkt Hans, "dot de

shildren in der Tyrol are mosdly fery well pehaved."

"Dot comes," reblied der Professor, "pecause dere is so many *Popanze* or *Boogaboos* or dings dot deir Mutters frighten dem mit, to make dem pehafe. Vhere de shildrens is pecome Agnostiker and tont believe in pug-bears, und are not horror-strook und terrorised und shooked mit awe at idèal phantoms—as in America—dere dey are all de paddest vons ash you can find. *Ja wohl.* Dough inteed we hafe not soosh a tremendous lot of *Kinderschrecker* as dey hafe in Ungarn, as you may read in de fery inderestin' articles written by Ludwig Kálmány.[1] For dere dey have a *Popé*, der *Arkus-Barkus*, der *Bubus* und *Mumus* und *Lele* und *Mokan* mit efer so many more—ja de shildren in Hungary most pe fery goot—if dey surfife it!—— Howefer, we hafe cot a goot many of de same sort of scare-crows or scare-boys among oos as you may yoodge from dis story."

[1] Given in *die Ethnologische Mitteilungen aus Ungarn*. Budapest. Edited and published by Anton Herrmann.

Germany—Tyrol.

Denn der Professor telled his legend, und der Breitmann was so compressed mit it, dot he singed it in rhyme as vollows—indo a boem :

HIES'L.

Dis is a tale of de tays of oldt,
Of Gratsch, a blace in de wild Tyrol't.

Hies'l of Kircherhof, on de Green,
Was der worst liddle poy dot nefer vas seen ;
Vot beoples calls a *Gassenbub'*
Dot roons on de shtreets a-rollin' a hoop,
A whistlin', a shkreemin', or trowin' shtones,
De kindt vot parents looks at mit groans ;
De poys dot vherefer dey com' mit deir fun,
De togs all park und de Katz all run ;
Gott keep all Vaters und Mutters bof'
From shildren like Hies'l of Kircherhof !

Von tay his Mutter : " Mein Hies'l," sait she,
" Dou moost try for a petterer poy to be,
Und keep from dis trowin' shtones—und squarrels,
Und do dein pestest to mend dy morals :
Und ven de Ave Maria bell rings
At evenin', stay home like averydings,
Und don't go blayin' in efery alleys,
Mit all de vagapond Toms und Sallys ;
For 'tis well pe-known, ash all remark,
Dere are dreatful Dings vot browl in de dark

Dere's de *Schreckenhund* so plack und crate,
Mit eyes of fire ash bick ash a plate;
Und die *Grüne Hexe*—de green oldt witch—
Vot go for all pad liddle poys mit a svitch;
Und die *Frau von Hitt* vot ride on a horse,
Und carry dem off in a sack of course;
Und der *Käsemannlein* vot look like sheese,
Doot coots deir lecks short off at de knees;
Und die *Norgen* who alvays deir work pegins
Py prickin' pad poys to deat' mit pins;
Und der *Eismann* vot grap 'em und nefer shtop
Dill he carry dem off to de mountain-dop,
Und poonishes all deir grimes und vice
Py toornin' dem into loomps of ice.
Likewise der derriple *Wilder Mann*,
Vot skhare 'em to deat' so moosh ash he kann;
Und die *Grosse Trude* vot live in de fiel's,
Boot com' indo town pad poys to shteals;
Und die *Wasser Fräulein* vot rise from de lake
Und gifes dem bieces of pies mit cake,
Und dakes dem all from de land or shore,
Und dey nefer peholds deir Mutters no more,
So doun in *das Wasser* dey haf' to shtay
Vhere she vips und vollops dem efery tay;
Und der *Orgo* dot mak't de shildren fare ill,
For he has a mout' as pig ash a barrel;
Dere into der same soosh kinder he stecks,
Und eat 'em all oop exgsep' de lecks :—
'Dis a terriple sight—dot mout' so wide
Mit de lecks of shildren hangin' outside!

Germany—Tyrol.

Und der *Pechmannerl* so derriple, vitch
Has haar so plack dot it shine like pitch,
He com' to beoples mit a shmile
Boot is pent on killen 'em, all de vhile ;
Und die *Wichtelmänner*, or liddle elfs,
Dot is fery moosh like bad poys demselfs,
Und are always tryin' de same to fix
Mit some kind of gruel und efil dricks ;
Und der *Pütz'l* or *Butz*, vot trow you mit shtones
Und shen'rally ents by preakin' your pones ;
Und der *Neckgeist* dot mocks und jeers so pad,
Who shneers you alvays dill you go mad ;
Und der *Fanga* dot cotch you mit a charm
Und garry you off all oonder his arm ;
Und die *Waldfräuleins* mit de *Willeweiss*,
Mit die *Wilde Dirne*, dot in a drice
Fly away mit poys to a tisdant shore ;—
Dere is all of dese—and a hundert more,
Dot will surely cotch you—my Hies'l—mark !—
If you roon apout in de shtreets py dark."

Boot der Hies'l gared not a pin—not he—
For all his Mutter's Mytologie ;
Nay—he dinked he wouldt like to hafe a looks,
If dey coom in his way, at som' of dese *spooks*,
So now you shall hear how dis ding he tried,
Und how his tesire was sottisfied.

Dot fery efenin' ash shtill ash a mouse
Dis Hies'l sofdly shdeal from de house—

Foorst of all—ash de Glock' shtrike Elf'—
A biece of fruit-bread—and denn himself,
Und shlip out of toors, und denn pegun
A loafin' apout to look for fun,
Like many olders who'd petter keep
Demselfs in deir Betts und go to shleep,
Dill all of a sutten der poy tid note
Yoost near pefore him a peaudiful goat,
A fine plack goat right dere in de *Eck'*
Mit a pell a ringin' around its neck.

" Hooray ! " cried Hies'l—" de game's pegun,
Mit dot Goat I'll go it—und hafe some fun.
A goat is ash goot as a pony to ride."
So oop on de Billy he gets ashtride,
Und sure ash you live—for id all is drue—
Avay like a race-horse de onimal flew,
Und der Hies'l, telighted, gry out, " Hip, ho !
Dis is de vay for a veller to go ! "

Ven he mark dot dis Goat—dot vas plack ash a nigger,
Pegan to enlarge und crow visiply pigger,
Und ash it crew pigger pegan for to vly
Ofer de Houser und oop to de sky,
Afay, afay in de silentzed night,
Dill Hies'l cot horrored und shkreem mit fright,
Und vished he nefer had goned out blayin',
Und vas safe in his Bett mit his home acain !

Germany—Tyrol.

Now Hies'l, his Mutter, had long pegun
To veel fery ooneasy apout her Sohn;
She knowed dot his dricks und his little vays
Wouldt pear a watchin' py nights or tays;
So vhen she had foundet he'd left *das Haus*,
She caught oop her ponnet und busted heraus,
Und rooned ash if led py som' shpirit or shtar,
Along de roads in de fields afar,
She know'd not whidder—she wist not where,
Like a bird dot is whirled on a shtorm troo de air,
Or a flock of schnow, or a hoonter's dart,
Vhen Someding a soodenly maket her start!
For she heardt far ofer her het a gry;
She lookt und peholdet abofe in de shky—
Ach Himmel! vot sights for a Mutter to note!
Her Hies'l a-ridin' a Billy-goat!
She trilled mit de horribelest alarms,
Her shpirit was shlog mit teadly squalms,
Yet e'en in dot instinct of vild tespair,
She ootered a brief-compacted brayer,
Yoost "*Ave Maria!*"—no more in fac',
Vhen der Goat trow'd Hies'l off of his pack!

Off like an arrow ge-shot from a pow—
Boot ha!—dere's an Oak-dree a crowin' pelow!
He is safed—he is won! *Donnerwetter*, vot yoy!
For de pranches shoot out und cotch holt of der poy!
Like hands mit fingers dey clasp him soft,
Und Hies'l is helt py de dwigs aloft,
Und die Mutter look oop—und vot did she see
Boot der Hies'l a-schwingin' on dop of a dree!

Hans Breitmann in Germany.

Von Chronik say dot, "*Es ist wahr*
Sie holt ihn herab mit Lebensgefahr":
Dot means dot de brave und tefotet Wife
Did glimp und safe Hies'l py riskin' her life;
Boot anoder teclare dot de beoples in town
Coom oop mit a latter und rescued him down.
I cannot say vitch—id vould vex a Saints
To settle so many Chronic gomplaints.
All dot I know, twas py Huber-Ried
Dot Hies'l was caught py der dree, inteed,
Und a liddle chapel was pilt dere, to show
Dis dings vot hoppen'd so long aco,
Mit a peautiful carvin' in which de folk
May see Hies'l a shtickin' on dop of de oak,
Mit a Gōtic-Latin inscribtion vot shtate,
It dook blace in Twelf hundret und Forty Eight.
From vitch I inver—und I write it mit yoy,
Dot Hiesl' reform't to a fery goot poy,
Und berhops in dime comed into a Saint,
Dough for dis I'll not schvear dot he is or he ain't.

Now all liddle poys—if dis meet your eye,
(Und also some pigger vons py de py),
Yoost learn from it de Trūt' vot I dell,
If you mind your Mutter you'll alfays do vell,
For in avery dings id is cerdainly drue—
Your Mutter knows pest vot is goot for you,
For mit all de visdom dis vorld enyoys,
De Mutters know pest how to manage de poys,
Vedder dey're meant to pe briests or laymen:
Gott keep dem all in his mercy. . . . Amen!

CHAPTER II.

ON DE GIGANTIC VIRDUE OF GERMAN PATIENCE,
MIT DE HISTORIE OF GERMAN GIANTS IN TIROL.

"Pazienza disse il lupo al asino."
"Pazienza vince Scienza."
"Patientia, tempus, pecunia
Will put any discord in tune-ia.
Patentia, patientium,
Said Saint Antonium."
Italian Proverbs.

"In Comitatu Tyrolensi prope Oenipontum (Innsbruck) est monasterium nomine Wiltavium, in quo ostenditur Gigas ingentis, et stupendæ magnitudinis nomine Haymon. Cujus sepulchrum pedes quindecim longum, leganturque ibidem intercæteros hi versus

Supra octingentos à Christi et septuaginta
Annus et octavus cum moreretur, erat
Vnde vides grandem tumuli sub imagine formam,
Ex ligno prisco quam posuere patres,

Aspice ferrato regem dormire cubili,
Corpore quod cubitos æquat atroce novem."
De Gigantibus (*In Miraculia Vivorum, auctore
Henrico Kornmanno*, A.D. 1614).

DE Tyrolers are all a bleasant, yolly, gootnadured, glean, *gemüthliche* folk—*deswegen*, or derefore, all their downs und fillages hafe a friendly outlook, for id ist alfays visible vot beoples ist like, ven you sees how dey *life*, und how dey keep deir homes. Yoost ash in Italy dere is alvays somedings *schlotterig* und *schlumpig*, or loafery, slummy und slumpy apout de shdreets und houses, mit all deir peauty, so de Tyroler views, or onsights, are onvariaply neat mit romandic elegance, pecause mosd of the volk talks Deutsch ven anypody ist lookin' on, und gopples Italienisch 'mong demselfs ; dot is a kind of *Kauderwälsch* vot vouldt have droved Petrarch indo fits mit all his knowingness of Italian *Dialecte*. Und ven der Herr Breitmann comed indo de Marie Theresien Strasse, he trowed oop his het like an ox trow oop his horns ven he coom to a hill, und exglaim : "*Donnerwetter !*—dot is vot I lets undo mineself pe called wonder-

Germany—Tyrol.

shiny peaudiful!"—for he moost allow dot in all his drafels he hat nefer seen a more preddier *brosbectus*.

Dis Strass' is so breit dot id sees out more like a *Platz* or *biazza* dan a shdreet, und de lines of houser on eider site is made of pildings vitch ven not *palastartig* or paladial, are all-dings foorst rate painter-ish, und lets demselfs coom indo fiews for de opera. Yoost in de Mitte dere heaves idself up de Anna-Säule, a colomn of red Tyroler marple—vot tower on high mit a *Muttergottesbild*, like it would lift de Madonna oop to heafen.

> As if id vould soar oopward
> In de evening-cloudy glow;
> Vile castin' a shadow townvards
> Oopon de folk pelow!

In dot *Weg*, Breitmann bewoondered die Spital-Kirche, vhere dere is a *Predigt* or breaching in Italian afery Sunday, und going-ofer or opposite a lordtly house whereon is a boost of der poet and musiker der crate Herrman von Gilm.

"*Da liegt ein Musikant begraben,*" say der Breitmann, "ven nod in der pody, *doch* yet in der spirit—ven nod in de field, boot *stättlich* or stately in der *Stadt.*" Dere too he peheldt de Ottenthal House und de *Landhaus* constroocted py Anton Gump. " Dat ist de virst dime," said der Breitmann, " dot I efer heardt of a crate Gump vot do anyding clefer ! "

All aroundt und afar und peyond on high, rosed a fringe of shnow-tipt moundains, vot seem so nigh und yed so far—even vile de Sonn' is hot in de shdreets, und oldt vomen is selling beaches und figs on der corners. So ein dirsty, weary Deutscher lets dem daste goot to himself ven he coom across de Alpen into so ein golden *Fruchtenland* or fruit-land.

Also vas he let himself be bleased mit de *Fruchtenbrod* or fruit-bread vot you see in all de baker-cake shops. Dis is gomposed mit rosins, ficks, almondts, pine-kernels, und pits of fery hard shweet stoff, paked in a croost, mit shpice und sugar. De English beoples dink it dastes like a handfoll of crabble-shtones gemixt mit molasses, or prown sugar—but de Deutschers und

Germany—Tyrol.

Tyrolers lofes id all de same as mintz-py, und calls it *Engelbrot* or angel-pread. *Ja*, der crate Hungarian joker Moritz Jokai say in a romance dot de folk in Hungary bities the oder beoples in de lands vhere *Fruchtenbrod* is unbeknown, und voonder vot yoy dey can find in life mitout id.—For *de gustibus non est disputandum*, dere is no use in squirreling about daste—dough I gonfess I findt it hardt to pelieve, ven I hear dot dere is in dis vorldt beoples vot ton't love *Sauerkraut*, nor caviare. Vell-vell!—so id goes!

> Ei'm jeden gefällt seine Weise wol
> Drum ist die Welt der Narren voll.
>
> [All beople dinks deir own taste sound,
> Derefore do fools so moosh apound.]

"Und de moral of id ist, dot we moost all hafe *Geduld* or patience mit von anoder.

"Only, ton't garry batience too far. Vonce oopon a dimes dere vas a Dootchman vot missed de *Lichtputze* or candle-snoofers. He hoonted all ofer de haus, boot couldn't find dem. All dot day he vos a snoofer-less Dootchman.

"Ven de Night coom on, he sot toun und

saidt : 'All tay long I cot some liddle crabble-shtones in mine poot, I kess I'll dake dem out.'

"So he sot toun und pooled off his poot, und helt it oopside doun—und poured out de snoofers! He hat peen trodden on dem in his poot all-day.

"Dis Dootchman hat too moosh *Geduld*, or more batience dan was goot for him. Id were goned him petter if de virst ding early in de mornin', ven he veel de candle-snoofers a hurtin' his foot, he hat cot mad und saidt : '*Potz Höll*' *und Teufel! vas ist* in mine sole?' und pooled de poot off, und took de light-shears out. For dere vas alvays somedings *riesengross* or pig as shiants in de Deutschers, of all kind und sorts, und dis veller hat shiant patience. *Ja*—ve trink like shiants, und vork und vight—*ja*—und *soofer* like dem. Ve pe's fery ofden somevot *ungeholfen* or glumsy, und to-whiles ; or now und den ; rader *dumm* (dot is, shtupid)—boot id ist like a shiant and nod like an Italian monkey. Ash der crate Johonnes Hinkelbeinius scibed in his *Topographie* of *der German Soul*—'Id ist petter to pe pig like a vild boar dan liddle like a Maus.' De

Germany—Tyrol.

Deutschers may pe like vild-Bores und Shiants, boot nefer like mices."

Dis vos the reflections of der Breitmann ash he coom into de Hofgasse und peholded ash he elefated his eyes, *das Riesenhaus*, or House of der Shiant, vot coom like a Wonder-work of intuning, or go-inside-ence mit his dinking. For vot he saw vos a Middle-elterly house mit de sdatue in shtone of a Goliath in armour, fery vonderful to fiew, und py de side of id vas a tablet mit de following vorts :

> DIS HOUSE
> DER ARCHDUKE SIGISMUND OF TIROL PILDED
> IN DE YEAR 1490 FOR HIS SHIANT NIKO-
> LAUS HARDL, UND HAT DE SAME
> MIT HIS IMAGE ADORNED.

De Tyrol vas alvays famous for Shiants, even so for fery pick, handsome men to dis tay. Dere ist ladies in Vienna, *sogar Hofdamen* of de topmost arisdocracy, vot pay *enorm* brices for yung Tyroler Colasseses, vot dey are so *unverschämt* as to geep apout deir bersons like bett-lamms, so crate is de *luxuria* and vicketness of dis vorldt. Und in de fifteent' year-hundred dere vas still a crate deal of *Aberglaube* und soaperstition remainin' apout dem, vitch is de reason vy der Duke Sigismund und Ferdinand II. revardet deir shiants mit shblendid houses, und sdatues, vitch vos more dan dey vould hafe efer don for any shiants of Intellect dot efer lifed, vitch shows dat it is petter to pe porn a seven-footer dan a heaven-porn Sohn of genius.

De vay dis Soaperstition coom apout, vas, dat in de oldt dime, so long for-bey ash never vas, de Tyrol vas so fool of dese pig vellers, dat id moost hofe peen de *Haupt-quartier* und fater-land of all de Shiants, of de fery tallest und brutallest kind. Und die *Historia* bescribe dat among dese vas der Glunkezer Riese ; or Shiant ; die Albacher Riesen, der Dornasser Ries', Riese Gauner, also Heims, Thürse, de Vintschgauers, der Salvenjoch und Marbachjoch, und der Schwarzegger.

    Soosh is de nople Historie,
    Of de Shiants vot lived on the mountains free,
    Dot mit deir teeds so gross und grand

Germany—Tyrol.

Erstaunisht de Volk of avery land,
Mighdy in form mit awfool face,
De Vaters of our German race.

Und derewith der Riese, or Shiant, von Tschsiersthal, vot vas so *enorm* dot ven he vos ashleep und shnorin', beople dink id vas *Donner*, und all de more so, pecause his breat' plow de drees like a dempest all a-doun. Now all of dem have got deir *Biographias* in de Sagas of Tyrol, und among dem dere is dis apout der Schwarzegger Riese, showin' how he come to grief :

DER SCHWARZEGGER SHIANT.

All in der Haufenwalde, und in der mornin' dime,
Vere men a pildin' houses mit shtein und wood und
    Leim ;
Oont ash dey lay de dimpers shoost ash der meister
    bid,
Dere coom an oldt cray *Riese* vot looked at vot dey
    did :

He say undo de beople : "*Ich denke diesen Wald,*
Ich denke ihn auf Ehre—neunmal jung und neunmal
    alt :
Dot means he could rememper dot forest und de
    wold,
Ven it vas nine dimes growing, und nine dimes ven
    d'was old.

Hans Breitmann in

But long ash I hafe peen here I nefer yet did see
A shiant or an anyding vot could ge-conquer me ;
You may dink you're mighdy clefer, but dis is fery drue,
I couldt sendt you all to donder if so I chose to do."

Hard py dere stoot a parrel, 'tvas full of water clear,
Id gave de vorkmen drouple to bring das Wasser dere,
Der shiant he vas dirsty, for him 'tvas boot a sup ;
He shdick his het in der parrel, und trink das Wasser oop.

Denn he said, " I'll coom to-morrow, again, und you you moost dink,
Efery tay to fill dot parrel dot I may take a trink :
Und if you do neglect id—look out for shdicks und shtones :
For denn, by Donnerwetter ! I smashes all your pones !"

De garpenters und puilders ge-bromist all he ask ;
Dey schvear to pring dot wasser vouldt pe deir daily task ;
Und dey kep' deir word *wahrhaftig*, bot dey vere glefer chaps,
Und dey truly fill de parrel—but dey fill it oop mit *Schnaps*.

Das schmeckte aem Schwarzegger, he like it you conceive ;
He nefer hat trink *Branntwein* before, I do pelieve :
He roll his eyes in ropture—he noddle mit his het,
Denn on de ground roll ofer so drunk like he vas tead.

Germany—Tyrol.

Dere vas a bully butcher by-standing mit an axe,
Und at de Shiant's necke he give an awful whacks,
Er haute den Kopf vom Rumpfe—he chop dot het avay;
Dere like a shtock or *Stumpfe*, mouse-dead dot Shiant lay.

Dis is de ancient legend, gesung ash you moost know,
All in de *Deutsche Wälder* a tausend yar ago:
Vitch show dough Demprance beople den Branntwein may apuse:
Dere somedimes coom a grysis ven it may pe of use!

"*Ja wohl*," say der Herr Professor, as he sat mit dem Herrn Breitmann in de Riese Tavern in de Hofgasse of Innsbruck, before der on-the-wall-painted portrait of Rainer the Tyroler Musician who by Heine be-mentioned is — "*ja wohl*—when I dink dot dis Hause to the last of de crate race of Tyrolese Shiandts pelonget have — denn I veel a vild Historic Durst me over-shteal, which me insbires his healt' to trink. *Ja* — ven we dink of de *Gigantes* of Old, de Nephylim and Rephaim of Genesis und Josua—of der Og—who was de first person who efer tropt an H—of Arba '*homo magnus inter Anakim*,' Pallas, Andromedas, Bohemus, Boiogero, Cormoran, und de hundreds of more Collossi who have into deat' away ge-passed—I wonder whet'er de human race inteed improvin' is? But forget not dot efen here in dis fery town of Innsbruck—known of yore as Oenipontum—dere lie be-buried, de Shiants Haymon und Thyrsus—dot is in de Kirch of Wilten—of whom dere is enough narrated a crate Buch to make. For in Thyrsus or *Turs*, or Anglo-Saxon *Thyrs*, we hafe of de Norse Jötun one of de cratest. Und I dink mineself dot dis is de same as *Durst* or *Thirst* which is de most enormous of German human bassions, und vitch tower apofe all our oder Teutonic faculties und endowments like a Catedral-Dom apofe de liddle houser down pelow. Und Haymon, accordin' to de Sympologists is from de Hebrew *Chayes* or Life or Appetite—dot is to say *Hunger*—soosh as we at noon exberience when we *Bratwurst mit Sauerkraut*, or Roost Schinken mit *Kartoffel-Salat* us pefore shmell— und berhabs a goot soup see. Und when dis de *Fall* is, denn all de humanly race moost atmit dot Haymon und Thyrs, or Hunger mit Durst, were truly of all our German ancesdors de fery cratest—*ja sogar* de noplest—und de feinest vellers ash nefer vas.

"Beople may say dot mit dem we are curst,
 Boot dere's really no plessin's like Hunger und Durst,
 For wert not for dem vhen dey binch us sefere,
 Ve'd nefer want vittles nor call for our Bier:
 Nor gare for a panquet, a shbree or a feast,
 Und pe lower in fact dan de prutallest peast,
 Ja—ve'd nefer ged dipsy—und dot peyond toubt
 Ish too awful a dings to pe dinkin apout.

"*Nun, gut*—in de yar 860 dere comed, ash some say oop from Italy, but ash petter sources brove, down der Rhine, a Deutscher giandt-nopleman, dwelf foot, four inshes high. Und de monchs cot holt of dis bully-big animal und benefolently him, not into bacon boot unto Christianity converted. Und dey galled him HAYMON afder de oldt Story of de Giant Hunger dot conquer Averypodies.

"Now yoost a few miles afay in dem Obern Innthal, dere lifed a sholly old Shiant named

Thurs, or Thurst—dough he was nod — as I sospose—de first, but of de name an inheritor only.

"Vell den—Honger der Christian und Durst der Heathen, one mit anoder to squarrelin' gecome were, und as Haymon was only 35 yar *alt*, poor olt Thyrs gekilt got. Von tay dey met py de Seevelt, on a prook dot is yet called de *Thursenbach*. Und de blood of Thyrs is yet dere on de red shtones to pe seen.

"Denn it to bass comed dot Haymon dis murder repentet—dot is he hat an awful *Katzenjammer* or hetache mit sorrow, afder extinguishin' poor olt Durst. Howefer de monks a goot way found it to work-off, und him useful to make.

"Dey say to him, 'Herr von Haymon, here py are de ruins of de oldt Roman city of Veldidena. Subbose you go to work und a cloister mit a church build—denn you all dis treadful murder will forgifen pe.' So der Haymon he coes at it, und de foorst ding he knowed he boorsted into an old Roman vault in vitch a mighdy Drack, or Dragon, vas house a-keepin'.

Germany —Tyrol.

Denn dey had an awful fight—*remis velisque*—toot' und nail—schofel mit tongs—ash is all in a vearfully long boem tescriped — dot reads as rackin' und ash rough ash a mountain-torrent bett ven you use id for a foot-road. Now Haymon de Drack gekilt, und puildet de Kloster und died in de yar 878. Und dere vas inscribet on his tomb an *Epitaphium* witch abbear to hafe peen written in de same measure und to de tune of—

> "'A lofely Maid to gonfession came,
> To a Friar von mornin' early.'

Und dis is de Scription.[1]

> "'EPITAPH.

> "'Ven a year und a tay had bassed away,
> After de yar Eight-hundred ;
> In Seventy-eight—dot vas de date,
> At Haymon's deat' we wondered.
> This hero pold, ash we are told,
> Tid build in dis blace a cloister,
> Gave his all 'tis drue, und serfed in id too,
> Yet wouldt not pe its Master.

---

[1] "Als Tag und Jahr verflossen war
Acht hundert schon verstrichen."
Inschrift des Begrabnisses.

Hans Breitmann in Germany.

>Lived well till he died—for Virtue tried,
>All pride und fanity hoompled,
>Boot anyhow—he's not livin' now,
>Since indo dis grave he toombled.
>   *Requiescat in Pace!*'"

"*Nun,*" rebly der Breitmann, "mine sympathies are radder more mit Olt Durst, or Thyrs, dot der Hayman killed did—*Kellner noch ein Glas!*—boot *ennihau*—dey were bote fine Kerls—

>"All goot vellers—I hafen't a toubt;
>Dis a bity de Race is tyin' out.

Der Hayman abbears to hafe peen somedings like der Sankt Christopher—Well!—here's to bot' deir healt's—und may deir shattows nefer lesser crow!—Gott pless 'em!"

CHAPTER III.

ON DE HAPIT OF SHTARIN' AT STRANGERS—DENN ON TREATIN' PEOPLE AS FOOLS UND ITS CRATE DANGER. DE BALLADE OF NARR-HANS'L.

> " Quum in aula venio
> Gaudent omnes, et non ego;
> It is dreatful dings to see
> Hou dey all do shtare at me."
> LUMP VON GAUNER, A.D. 1306.

WAS it efer hoppen to de Reader in de coorse of his happy or oonhappy life—(I kess it is peen a gemixture of de two)—to come suttenly pefore a cage vot condain two or tree dutzen Owls? He might hafe done dis ding vonce on de Peerless Pier of Brighton vhere dere vas a mann vot kept an Owlery.

Or vas der same Reader efer enter de preakfast-room of der Grand Hotel in Paris—or any oder such blace—ven two or tree dutzend Angular-Saxon beoples of all sorts und gonditions were engaget in destroying tea mit toast, ecks mit pacon, or café?

In eider case der man moost have opserved how all at vonce tree dozen pair—dot is sixty-four single eyes were all a-glarin' ot him like he vas an *Eindringlicher Störer*—a disturbin' intruder, as if to say, " Vot teufel pusiness you got here?"

Der crate artist und nofelist Du Maurier have made a *Punch*-bicture of a similar scéne—where de travel-worn und half-sick people are comin' from de Channel shteampoat—und de ladies und gendlemen at Dover crowd round to stare at dem ash dey com' to land.

Dere is not so moosh of dis shbirit of oonprovoked hosdilidy apparent in Deutschers or Frenches—pecause all dese beoples life so mush in hotels, und mofe apout so moosh more all de dimes in cafés or gartens, or in shmall dravellin', dot de endrance of an unbeknown, suddenly,

Germany—Tyrol.

vhere dey are eatin', does not erstonish dem und awake de veelin' of tisturpance, *und of pein' wronged*, dot all Englanders veel oonder de circumstances. Acain der Englander himself radder likes to coom in und pe gestared at und holt oop his het poldly mit a sub-feelin', vitch if developet wouldt say: "You all go to *Donner* mit yourselfs, und shdare as moosh ash you tam blease!" Dis is nod foolly *ausgesprochen* or ooterly ootered—id ist only *in petto*—but id ish *dere*. Id is a kind of excitin' exhilaration pattle—yoost ash *Gassenjunge* or shtreet poys like to sling sass at von anoder ven dey meed, for de sake of victory.

Now, on de oder hand, if a man pe a *Deutscher*, und esbecially in some cornerland vhere Touristic or English influences hafe nod benetrated, und beople ist not as yed cultured into incivilidy, or cifilized into boorishness—vhen dot man cooms indo a *Kneip* or café, or sush dings, de beoples greets or salutes him mit boliteness und vishes him a *guten Appetit*—und denn und dere dey do somedings to make him *veel at home*. Und if dot comer-in vas at vonce to broseed to dell dem vot he had yoost seen while a-comin'—or vhere he coomed from—or vot woonderful dings he efer met mit anyvhere—or norate a fairy-tale—'dis all von——if id bleased dem dey vould only like him all de petter—so dey got deir fun somehow.

Now as among Englisch beople dere is some assemplies vot glare mit more fiendishness or inimicality at intruders, und also some men vot coom in mit a pigger headt of sass und cheek on dan oders——so, *im Gegentheil*, or on de gontrary, dere are *Deutsche* assemplies; specially among rural folk; who are more sympathetisch-cifil dan oders vhen an unbeknown enders on de Scéne—und also (as it oonderstands idself) some men who ven dey come in to soosh assemplings—*ei!*—'dis like de comin' of a favouride actor on de sdage—averypody shmiles—dere is a booz of bleased *Anticipirung*. . . .

Now I moost dell you dot der Breitmann vas yoost von of dis ladder sort of vellers as nefer was . . . dere pein in his whole exbression a sort of *Zeitgemässigkeit* vot insbire de veelin' ash if he had *yoost com' at de right time*—und nod (as mit

Germany—Tyrol.

de Englisch), ash if he had intrudet at de wrong von. Und id coom to bass dot in de town of Bingen in der Tyrol, he endered a *Wirthshaus*, in de *Stube* or puplic-room of vitch dere sot a compagnie of resbecdaple beoples vot seem to pe *ungemein heiter*, und dey greetet den Hans mit so mooch *génial* consiteration dot he veel like dey vas all affecdionate relations met to celeprate his gebirth-day.

Now ven Hans had told dem all mitout mush ceremonie vot his name vas, und vhere he coomed from, mit so moosh of his Biographie as might cheer de oldts und encorage de yungs—und inderest dem all connectively, he ashk vhere dere vas a goot *Herberg* or lotchin-house—nod too egspensife—a *privat* decent blace.

Dereat de oldest inhapitant of de room sent oud a poof of shmoke—like ash von fires off a bistol pefore de horses shtart in a race—und pegin :

"Dere ish a fery goot und *ehrlicher* Mann hier in Bingen dot hafe cot a shmall haus mit tree *Zimmer* or goot rooms vot he let out sheap—*aber Schad'*—dis a bity dot you had not coom dere ten yars sooner vhen dere vas anoder wirth, und knowed vot a veller knowed dot lived dere."

" *Wie so*—how vas dot?" inquire der Breitmann, ash he refreshed himself mit anoder glass of bier.

" *Nun*—dis is de shtory :—vot is all ash drue ash several seven Bibels mit a Catechism troun in. *Zehn yars* by gone, dere coom to dot liddle *Logis* a *Fremder* a foreigner of some sort—*Gott weiss was!*—some dinked he vas a Ungar, und some a Böhme, und some a Roumanier—but votefer he vas he had blenty of money, und gueer fancies. Foorst he pay to hafe all das Haus painted green mit his bicture on it . . . denn he cot a wood-carver to make a Bild or a Image of a girl, vot he had coloured like life—and poot it a-looking oud of der window—shoost like dere vas a gal dere—mit a peautiful golden *Haube* or cap—fery wundervoll to pehold——*ja*—und *Gott weiss was* for *wilde Grillen* or sdrange fantasies dot man didn't hafe. Und all de dime his

Germany—Tyrol.

landlordt dink he was a *Narr* or a fool, und say *Ja* to averyding, und make him bay dwice as moosh ash he ought to for his *Ideen*.

"*Nun, gut!*—von tay der *Hausgenoss* or lodger say to der *Wirth* dot he moost hafe de whole house to himself for von mont', pecause he always bass dot dime efery yar in prayer und fastin' all *allein*, und dot he pray all night long on de bare ground, in de keller, 'cordin' to de rites of his holy religion.

"Denn der landlord knew der Mann was a heat'en vot foller de old soaperstition of de *Hexen* or witches, vot always maken deir brayers to de Spirits in *Kellers*, or in deep caverns, und all soosh *Larifari* und *Unsinn*, und nonsents. Howefer, so long as it payed money, der landlort was always ready *in Jemandes Horn zu blasen*—to join in mit any man's melodie. So he rentet das Haus for dree dimes more ash id was right to bay—und he laugh mit his friendts over dis *Dummkopf* of a man. Und dey watch de lodger, but all dey opserfe vas dat he seemed, as de sayin' is, to go

"Früh mit den Hühnern zu Bette,
Auf mit dem Hahn um die Wette."

[Early to Bett mit de hen,
Und rise mit de cock again.]

"Boot dis *Dummkopf*, ash dey dinked him knew *wie man sein Schäfchen ins Trockne bringen soll* — how to keep his sheeps dry, better dan he seemed to understand. *Ja*—und he *verstand die Passauer Kunst* — he hafe learned de trick of Passau — dot is to keep himself safe from all loss or harm."

"How was *dot?*" inquire der Breitmann.

"In de old dimes," reblied de ancient Inhabitant, "dot vas in de tays of King Olim —dere vere Men who knew how *sich hieb-stich- und kugelfest zu machen*—how to guard dem- selfs from cut, stab, or gun-pullets, und beople still say so of a veller dot knows how to dake goot care of himself.

"*Nun, gut*—pefore de mont' vas oop, der Mann vanisht—but no von minded it, pecause he had paid his rents in advance und made de landlord shwear nod to tisturb him. So de time flowed py, und ven de Monat vas oop, dey boorst open de door — and vot you dink dey found?"

"*Ja—was war's?*"

"Dey found an iron *Kist'—altgothisch*—fery fine of ids kind, in der keller. Und de ground had been digged all out efer so teep. Under de kist dere vos a script vot say:

"'MINE TEAR LANDLORD,

"I am a man whose ancestors vonce owned dis Haus. Among de familie parchmends I found von four hundred yar oldt, vot tell how mine *ur—ur—ur gross*-grandfater hafe gepuried hier an enormous *Schatz* of Gold. Not to hafe any law-suits or sharin de money mit you, or any droples, I yoost took *das Haus* for a month witch gife me all de rights—as de lawyers will dell you.

"'I hafe digged oop dis *Schatz*—und found it was more ash a pushel of gold coins mit oder dings of value beyont all gomputation. I vould hafe gifen you some of dis mit bleasure, or enof to make you rich—but I learn dat you hafe ofercharge me for de rent pecause you dinked I vas a fool, und laugh at me mit Averypodies. Derefore I leave you, *zum Andenken*, dis iron kist to keep your monies in.

"'Your Friend,

"' DER FOOL.'

"Dot was all dey found—except two or tree old gold monies lyin' apout. Und der mysderious Stranger nefer shined no more in dis city."

"Dat shdory," remark der Breitmann, "ist like de lizards vot somedimes hafe two tails—it has two Morals after id. De foost ist, dot it is fery unbleasant to lose a ding efen if we tid not know we had id. *Segondly*—He laughs pest who laughs de last—like der veller tid vot cot afay mit dem Gelt. Und on dop of dis I add dot you had alvays petter dink dwice before you make fun of a fool. For avery fool has four dimes as much mischief in him, und ten dimes more refenge dan a wise man, und derfore he is fourdeen dimes more likely to pay you

Germany—Tyrol.

oop und hafe it out on you. Let os trink!"

"Ja," reply a yung man dot look like a Student—"*Hüte Dich vor Narren*—peware of fools is an oldt proferb. Truly it would hafe peen goot for de gendlemen of der Town Council of Munich vonce oopon a dimes, if dey had minded it."

"Vot vas dot for a story?"

"*Nun*, it is a song, und mit your honouraple permission I will sing it."

Der Student dook down a guitar dot hanged on de window-side, und afder doonin' de shtrings, sang mit a goot voice de Ballad of

NARR-HANS'L.

Oh! Munich is a merry town—'tis writ py many a pen—
Und all its City-Councillors are wund'rous merry men,
Und vhen dey meet for panketting, to refel or to sing:
From de Rathshaus to der Frauenkirch, you hear die Music ring.

Und afery von hafe got a Squire dot on his Master wait,
To fill his beaker oop mit wein, or change or fill his plate,
Und it always was expected—like de chorus to a song—
He moost laugh at all his masder's yokes und help de fun along.

Now, von of dese attendants vas an odd fantastic wight,
You saw id in his features dot Someding vasn't right.
An anxious-solemn countenance mit sorrow interwrought
Like von who knows he's crazy-queer, und doesn't like de tought.

And if de beople vext him ven he'd had a little trink,
He vouldt rave und gry de maddest dings dot mordal man could dink ;
Und shkreem, und weep und peg dem all for mercy in his pain ;
Which make folk roar mit laughter, und pegin to tease again.

Dey called him der Narr-Hans'l — dot is Jack Lunatic,
Und all de Herrs resolfe von tay to blay dis Mann a drick,
So dey maket him eat a herring till he almost die mit Durst,
Und denn gave him Wein to squench it—but dot vas not de worst.

Germany—Tyrol.

For der Wein was all prepáret mit pepper for a trick,
Also mit medecíné—vot maket him deadly sick,
So dot he tantz apout mit pain und many a mad
  grimace;
It maket de noble gentlemen all roar to see his face.

Nun, gut—de fun was ofer und das Ding was half
  forgot,
Und acain dere vas a Panket held all in dot merry
  shpot,
Und all pecause Narr-Hans'l mak't soosh fun vhen
  last dey dine,
Dey have him for der Kellner or de Master of der
  Wein.

De Musik roared in merriment; dere all was Saus
  und Braus,
Till der Chair-man gave das Wort—*Schenk ein!*"—
  und denn de sign " *Trink aus!* "
Now dis was at de Ende vhen efery present Man
Must trink de Supernaculum—dot is trink out his
  Can—

To a drop oopon his dum-nail—nor leafe pehind a
  rest,
Und der Wein for dis last trinkin' was of de fery
  pest,
Avery coop-ful cost a florin, of dot dere vas no doubt,
It glow like golden Sonnlight vhen Narr-Hans'l poured
  id out.

Hans Breitmann in Germany.

Hei! Vot can pe de Matter mit dem nople President?
Dot he look so pale as ashes und extremely discontent?
Und now he's fallin' backwards in deadly agonie!
And now—by Gott!—de oders are all ash ill ash he!

Hei! Vot can pe de Matter mit Narr-Hans'l?—Troo it all,
He is laughin'—he is shkreemin'—he is tantzin in de holl,
He is changed indo a teufel—he make a comic sigh,
Und he blay upon de cittern ash he see de Herren die!

Dere are four-and-twendy tead Men a lyin' in de room;
De tapers burnin' lowly—all fadin' into gloom;
De Waiters mit der Musik have all in Terror fled,
Da sitzet der Narr-Hans'l a-singin' to de Tead!

A-singin' wailin' ditties all in de wildest strain,
How dey poison him mit Pepper und he poison dem acain,
Till he shkreems: " It all is ofer—und der Wein is of de pest——"
He trinkt a *vollen Becher*—he is lyin' mit de rest.

CHAPTER IV.

WHY DE GERMAN TOURISTS DO TELESCOPES CARRY. DE YANKEE GALS MIT A SPY-GLASS UND VOT DEY SAW! DE BALLAD OF KATRINA BAUER WHO DE PROFESSOR KILLED.

"And there a man mit a sphyglass fery interestin' tiscoveries can make."—HEINRICH HEINE, *Reisebbilder*.

VON of de dings dot Hans Breitmann shbeedily opserfe in Tyrol, was dat afery Sherman *tourist* alfays garry mit him a *Fern-rohr;* dot is a tallow-scoop, or opera-glass, dot hang py his site from a shtrop ofer his shoulter. Der Englander hafe one, somedimes, der Fräntschman occasionally, der Italiëner now und denn—but der Deutscher *immer* und invariaply.

Von efenin dere vas a Barty of travellers,

German, *sowie* English und Mericans, all gesembled togeder in der *Goldene Adler*, vitch is de oldst Guest-haus in Innsbruck I guess as nefer vas, like de *Drei Mohren* in Augsberg, vitch is a tausend yar oldt, vere de Crusaders used to poot oop. Und in dis Golden Adler, der Goethe und der Heinrich Heine, mit seferal oder Emperors und Kings eider in Literature or Geography, hafe gewoned. Und right opposite ist de Ottoburg, built by Otto, der Duke of Andechs in 1234, on vitch you may readt:

"Here de Ottoburg dot' stand,
A House oophelt in Gottes hand."

Now de gompany vas ask vy de Deutsche Touristen alvays garry opera-classes. Und der Breitmann shbeak dus:

"De reason for dis uncessant telescoping; I kess; is dot der Deutscher is nefer sotisfyed mit vot de eye dake in naturally, or mit de peautiful scenery vot he can see——he alfays vant to pehold dot vitch is *not* fisible und crasp de unforeseen Infinite. If he hafe in sight a moundain, mit cloudts a vlyin' ofer its snowy soomit

Germany—Tyrol.

like treams of yout' ofer de het of an old man shleepin'—und foaming dorrents rooshing doun its site, like vite silfer stripes down de green robe of an old Irish bard—denn der Deutscher vouldn't dink he hafe seen dot moundain at all —*keineswegs*, or no-ways, oonles he desgry mit de outmoost persbicacity all de stocks und steins, und dings, all ofer de *Gebirge*, und dis he gall '*accurat* perception.' Dus he carry a kind of pusiness-like habit indo all his art, und mit all his transcendentalism he vas alfays forget in studyin' *die Natur* dot half its peauty ist in opscuridy.

"Dis carryin' de opera-classes und also dis seen' dings a goot vay off, dot it vas yoost as vell to leave unvisiple; likevise dis unconsistent vant of logic; poot me mineself in mindt of de daughters of old Jacop Spraker a Dootchman-Hollander-New Yorker, vot life vonce oopon a dimes on de Mohawk Reservation on de Hudson river apofe Alpany.

"Von day der Spraker coom before der magistrate, und maket a crate morál gomplaint dot dere vas some unbrinciplet und shamelos yoong vellers, vot afery afternoon bathe und schwim in der rifer, mitout any dings on demselfs, rite in fool view of his taughter's vindows, und dot dis shkandalous spekdagle was fery moosh offend de motesty of de young laties.

"Der magistrat make inquiry of de beoples vot coomed for vitnesses, und found oud dot de blace vhere de yoong men bathed was a mile off from der Spraker his house.

"'How der teufel denn,' ashk der official, 'can dis trople your taughters, ven dey gannot dell, a mile off, vot dings vas fisciple in der rifer?'

"'*Ja*,' gry der Spraker—'boot mine gals has cot a pig delescope.'

"'Vell,' rebly der magisdrate: "I kess if dey vould do mitout dot delescope dey wouldt see yoost apout so moosh ash vas goot for dem.'

"Und dis ist ash drue for der Deutscher, und not de tourist alone, boot de whole breeds of dem in sheneral—dot dey would see yoost as moosh ash dey needs of Natur, or life, or de Peaudiful, mitout alfays a-telescopin' into averyding. Dere vas poets und ardists in de olden dime, vot hadn't

Germany—Tyrol.

any fieldt, or opera-classes, dot see a goot deal more in Natur dan de modérn Deutschers do mit all deir spyin'-tubes or far-pipes.

"Und dis lesson is goot not for Deutschers alone, boot for any oder man, pe he a Sprecher or a Spraker, or a Hollander—for ash de American Moral-Humourist opserved: 'I do not care if he pe an Amsterdam Dutchman—a Rotterdam Dutchman—or any oder d—m Dutchman—pecause I shbeak of de whole human races.'

"Boot id ist also vort noticin'—dat dis habit vot de Deutschers hafe cot, of alfays sückin' und searchin' for de *Unerreichbar* or Oonattainaple und de Mysderiös, and all de Infinightly opscurious dings, make it coom to bass dot dey also dake in de Serious mit de Comic, und de Sooplime mit de *Genial-gemein* or jolly-common, in a vay dat nopody else in de vorldt ever dinked of, und vot no oder beoples can *verstehn*, but vitch coom yoost ash natural to a Deutscher ash beer mit *Prätzels*. Und vot is more," gontinue der Breitmann, ash he glicked de *Deckel* of his mug as a sign to de maid to pring some more *Pilsener*—"dis ding enders into de life of de German, und id hoppen do him *alleweil;* all de dime ; like it hoppened to Nopody Else—ash befel de Katrina Bauer ven she fell indo de keller."

Here dere vas a general oudgry for de story. But der Breitmann dell dem id vas a song-tale or a ballade. Und virst he maket a *Vorrede*, or preamble, at a fast trot, dusly :

"You all know mine tear frents dot id ist a holy oldt gusdom in Germany, on de efenin pefore beople kits married, to holdt de sacred *Polterabend*, ven dey makes a row und kicks der teufel oop. Denn de folk kit togedder a lot of crockery-pots, or *Töpfe*, soosh as *Krüge*, eart'en *Geschirr, Theetischzeug* or tea-dings, *Kannen* und *Becher* vitch is moogs und yoogs, coffee-pods, *Bier-canone*, jars, pottles, flagons, noggins, dankards, bitchers, pibkins, long jorums, vot Nort' Deutschers gall *Jungfers,* or maidens—mosdly crocks of de sheapest und most ineffecdual kind soosh as is *crocked* alreadty."

Dis vas a bun, so de gompany all laugh bolitely.

"Dey kits de sheapest kind, pecause dese dings are only pought to be gebroken. Denn

Germany—Tyrol.

dey makes a *Teufel* of a hurly-purly shindy, und smoshes de grockery mit grys of '*Hei da!* *hep!* *yup!* *hoora!*' und dis dey gall *poltern*. Und in de Elsass de Fräntscher hafe de same gustom, und dey sings a pallad of de olden dime:

> 'Ohè! les petits agneaux!
> Ohè! les petits agneaux!
> Qui est ce qui caisse les verres?
> Qui est ce qui brise les pôts?'

Und de Deutschers sings too, for dere is a whole *fasciculus* or garland, or KRANTZ of dese lyrics, and I mineself hafe gontribute dis ballad to de total conglomeration."

Denn der Herr Schwackenhammer, who vas a fery goot *Clavierspieler*, sot doun ad de biano, und improfise a companiment, while der Breitmann sing in a teep *brumm-basso* vitch sountet like pumple-pees insite a drum:

DE BALLAD OF KATRINA BAUER.

Mit juch hei da! und *hop sa so!*
Am Polterabend wir waren froh,
For denn mit shticks so merry vere ve,
A-smashin' all de grockery.

Wir soffen Bier und Branntewein,
Wir schmissen alle de Fenster ein;
Dot means ve trinked de beer und gin;
Und smashed de vinders outside-in.

Mit "*Hägele! Krägele! Socker lot!*"
Katrina Bauer she proked a pot,
She proke de lid mit a hickory svitch,
Und call de bitcher "a son of a witch!"

Dere vas a Russian noble, vitch,
His name vas Mikel Sonnenovitch;
He dink Katrina call his name,
Und sofdly shmile oopon de same.

Und he sighed: "O Maiden fair to see!
Might I boot valtz a dantz mit dee!"
Katrin' foorst smash anoder pot;
Denn like der Teufel off dey shot.

Dey tantz so hard, dey tantz so sore,
Katrina boorst a hole troo de vloor,
She tantz so hard mit der Russian veller,
Dot bote her lecks shdick down in de Keller

Now ven der Russe look dereon,
Und see Katrina yoost half-gone,
Nod to let de 'casion shlip,
He shtoop'd—und shtole a giss from her lip.

Germany—Tyrol.

Now underneat' dis *Sturm'* und roar,
Dere sot a Deutsche Professor,
Ven Katrina's feets coom doun on his het,
Id shkared him so id kilt him tead!

All mit himself in de silendt night,
Dat lonely Student berish mit fright,
I know not if he die mit fits,
Or dink he vas *schläg mit donderblitz!*

Now a man may pe bote crate und vise,
Und fool of learnin' oop to de eyes,
Boot py shingo! id is more dan he can shtand
If a gal on dop of his het shouldt land.

So id goes in dis life—In numper Von
Dere is ofden noding boot shkreemin' fun;
Vile in de next—und dot is true,
Dere is *Deat'* mit derror, und all look plue—
Und ofden a gal connect de dwo!

Dereoopon dere vas a *Klatschen* or clopping of hands in uploudment of dis song, und von who vas bresent say:

"De idea of Katrina bein' gissed in roptures oop apove, vhile she ruptures de het of de professor toun-shdairs pelow mit her feets, is vot is called py der Rhetoricus an anti-thesis——"

Hans Breitmann in Germany.

"I shouldt rader say," rebly der Breitmann, "dot in dis case id vas an anti-*podes*, since dere vas a *Fuss* apout it."

"Halt dere!" gry de oder man. "Afder dot, I gife in—und shtand trinks all roundt. *Du Marie!*—dwelf glasses mit cigars!"

Und dey all trink to de healt' of der Breitmann.

CHAPTER V.

OF DE TOUN OF HALL, WITCH IS ALL PE-SALTED. HOW DER BREITMANN THIRSDY GOT, UND MADE LOFE TO DE PEAUDIFUL BEER GIRL. DE SHTORY OF GEORG'L, UND DE WONDERFUL BALLADE OF DER GOAT MIT DER SHPOON.

" Bacchus is ever to Venus dear,
For to set men to loving there's nothing like Beer."
Inscription in a Beer House in Heidelberg.

Now ven der Breitmann had beseeked und exblored de sights of Innsbruck, und seen all ids brincipal institudions vitch consist of de two rows of pronze statues in de Catedral mit Hofer's monument, das Museum, de Ambroser *Sammlung* vhere dey almost make more droples to see de dings mit dree *ciceroni* dan de show is wort, und de peautiful und vine Tiroler Hof Hôtel of Herr Landsee (vitch is de pestest in all

Austria), vhere der Breitmann lifed und wrote dis Buch, mit great gomfort und content, in a *Strudel* or Maelstrom or whirlpool gomposed of shwarms of Englisch und Merican tourists, all a goin' und comin' at vonce—remindin' Hans of a *Mühlgerinne* or mill-race dot he vonce see in America, vot consisd of dwo shtreams, von runnin' von vay und de oder anoder, owin' to de powerfoolness of de eddy!

Ven der Breitmann, ash I said, hat underseeked, or exblored, all dese mysderies, und made a *Serie* of *analytische-chemische*, or analytic-comical experiments mit test glasses, (vitch hold from a pint to a quart each), vitch result in de proof dot *das Bier* vas so goot ash Pilsener, denn he tooked his Alpenstock und Ränzel or knopsack, und vander all apout de land, to Berg-Isel, und Hall. Und ash he squander troo de lanes of dis pictureish andiquarian city, he pecame aware dot a derriple *Durst* vas shdealin' all ofer his foculties vot make him ash dry as de dust in July—or as a pone—or a baked mummy—or a hot brick—or a brush-maker—ven yoost ash his " sooferins pecame indoleraple

Germany—Tyrol.

und vere no longer to pe endured," ash an American president vonce set in a Message, he peheld a *Bier-garten* und rooshin' in, cryed for a doppelt pig glass.

Vitch ven he had schwallowed, Hans say to de fery nice gal vot prought de infusion of malts und hops:

"*Fräulein*—vot vas dot last remark I maket to you?"

De mädchen *lächelt* mit a shmile und ansver:

"Herr—you saidt: 'Bring me a dopple-glass of beer!'"

"Dot vas it," rebly der Breitmann. "*Keep* a pringin' dem. Successifely!"

De gal she prought von *Mass* of beer after anoder so fast dot she lookt like a procession goin' und comin', und der Hans empdy dem like he vas carryin' out a gontract to fill a fish-pond on time. Py und py he says:

"Holt oop for a minute pefore I boost—und dell me vot in name of de dry kings of Cologne id is dot maket me so dirsty so sooner ash immediadely ven I ender dis state of Hall, or Hell, —or votefer you call id!"

"*Ja, Herr,*" rebly de bier-maid, "*Wissens net?*—dot come from das Saltz where mit all die air, und aferydingt here ish imbregnatet. Und ash I vas teacht in de school, so ash to dell de outlanders und *Fremders* vot coom here, de fery name of the toun idself is Salt—pecause accordin' to de Tyroler historian, der fenerable Beda Weber, id cooms from de Greek *àlde* vot means Salt, vot vas brought from de Saline or salz-mines, vot is *annerthalb Stund,* or von und a half hour from here, dot costet fordy kreutzers to pehold. De drip affort nod only a sight of de Werks und grystal grottoes, *ganz wunderbar* to admire, so vine ash nefer vas, but also of romandic scenery mit climpses of de Speckahr, Bettelwurf, Nisselspitz und Schlingelschurkenspitzbubenschelmen-Alpe. *O ja, gewiss!* Denn dey pring de saltz here indo de city, mit de moral result dot de men are all as brackish ash brine und de women ash salt as Lot's wife. *O ja, gewiss!* Efen in de gonfersation of de gommon beople dere is somedings salty und racy, und bitin', und spicy, mit a bungency oonlike of oder folks. *O ja—gewiss! Daher kommt es,*—dence it resoolts all from de Saltz, dot der Hallers hafe all cot soosh a loose-speechfulness und ready tongueful-hood dot any von of dem *in fliessenden und tönenden Auseinandersetzungen ergeht über Dinge*—pours fort' his soul in torrent-like und loud teliferies ofer any dings at all, vedder he oonderstand dem or nod. *O ja, gewiss!*"

" All dot," say der Breitmann, "I do stetfastly peliefe ;—hafin de broofs pefore mine eyes, und esbecially hearin' dem in mine ears from you."

Now de *Mädchen* vas so inshbired und *begeistert* und corried avay mit her own oradory, dot she oonconsciously press oop to der site of der Breitmann, who ash undinkingly helt her py de hand to rebress her shweepin *Geberde*, or wavin' gesdures. Boot de fair orator not 'tendin to dis restraindt, vent on in full swing mit good elpow-room und a wide berth, free ash air und out of harness, as if her tongue vas all unbuttoned, unconfined, unchecked, unprefented, unhindered, unopsdructered, uncontdrolled, untrammeled, unsubject, ungoferned, unenslaved, emancipatet, unentralled, unreined, unpridled, uncurbed, unmuzzled, mit efer so many more uns and synonymes, vitch brove how crately de spiridt of de English language ist gifen to freedom—dere pein' more vordts in it vot exbress Liberty and Ease dan in all de oder languashes as nefer vas put togedder. Und de peautiful eloquentional *improvisatore* diffused as vollows:

" O ja, gewiss. De Saltz works is our crate industry, boot de peauty of our toun is our chief pride. Pilt oopon a hill-site, de shdreets forms a bicturesque compination of rural roats mit mittle-elderly *Gassen* or lanes, vot is faried mit oonexpegted ascensions und descents. O ja, gewiss ! From wide off de eye is *verhaftet*—dot is arrestet, or morally interestet, py a Gotic tower mit a red roof, und de griinish copper cuppelas of de Catedral vot vas pilt in one tousand zeven hundert-ein-und siebenzig, vot shouldt receive bewondering for de sake of ids vine Gotic pordal—its quaind relics—ids kloster vot vonce surroundet de *campo santo*—dot now obens on de ottroctife middle-efil walls of de Rathaus ! O ja, gewiss ! "

De maid vas so *entführet* or carriet afay mit

her own oradory und de peauty of Hall, dot she nefer nodice dot de shtalwardt arm of her auditor hafe vound idself round her bodice, und dot he 'peared to pe more apsorpet in her own peaudies dan in dose of de cidy. Boot dere vas *nopody in de garten yoost den*—vitch is a circoomstonts vot ofden maket a crate teel of tifference in many moral conjunctures ... und id vas rader mit a shmile dann a cross dat dis Hebe opserve vot had daken blace during her obsence of mindt.

So dot ven der Breitmann sofdly vispert: "*Gib mir emol a Busserl?*" ("Gife me a giss?") ... de gal glantz all roundt to see dat neider de oldt voman—nor any oder man—vas looking—und denn rebly:

"*O ja, gewiss.*"

* * * *

O, *Seeligkeit!* ... O *Wonne!* ... Vot dings id ish to pe a Lofer!

* * * *

Dere vas a Maiden fair und yung,
Who's soul vas like a shtar;
A Sorcerer feller comed along
Und shanged her to 'guitar:

Und ach ! vot wild und wunder dings
Troo all de *Seele* vent,
Vhen foorst mine fingers shwept de shtrings
Of dot strange Insdrument !

For in dot Musik of de Shpears
Vas more ash Melodie,
Und ach ! de Sound dot vill mein soul,
Vas more as Song to me ;
For more as Musik's last exdreme
Vas in dot tune I wot,
Und more ash Voice in deepest Tream
Vas in de Song, bei Gott !

Und ven dy Form oh Abend-Shtar !
Undo mine Hearts I shdrain,
Id seemt to me dot dot Guitar
Hafe got be-girled acain !
Und dot de Girl be-angeld is
Mit seraph-cherroops efen ;
Und Averydings in berfect pliss,
Is ropt afay to Heafen.

Und ven ve giss, mein shbirit vlies
To *Träume* far apove.
For dein are more dan mordal eyes,
Und dis is *more* ash Lofe !
For he who trinks as I hofe trinked
Das Bier ist more ash Wein ;
Und he who dinks vot I hofe dinked,
His Lofe pecomes difine !

* * * *

Germany—Tyrol.

Und yet wider . . . in de hoppy Tream.

LONG, LONG AGO.

Ven de pirds were singin'
 To de Summer preeze ;
Und de buds were flingin'
 Perfume from de trees :
  Hei da—ri dé !
  Hei da—ri do !
I sat py my Lofe so fair und gay,
All in de wood one Summer tay,
 Und *ach ! wir warn so frô.*

We sang oldt songs togedder,
 Songs of de merry dime ;
Und leicht ash any fedder
 We maket full many a Reim,
  Hei da—ri dé !
  Hei, da, ri laun !
Unto a lute we sang dis Lay,
Und so we passed de live-long Tay
 Undil de Sonn' went doun.

For efery song we pfluckt a Flower
 Und trowed it in de Grass ;
So you mighdt count before de bower,
 How many a lay dere was,
  Hei da, ri-dé !
  Hei da, ri-del !
Yed reckonet petter shdill dan dis,
 For to each ferse we put a kiss,
  Und kept de Count full well.

We sang oldt songs togedder,
  Of Loves long bassed away;
All in de bleasant wedder,
  Ash on de grass we lay:
    Hei da, ri dé!
    Hei da, ri dein!
No more can I rememper—yet
What I recall I'll ne'er forget
So long ash life is mein!

Denn der Breitmann wander onwarts—troo de wood lands troo de valleys—in de early mornin' Sonny-shine ven de rosy light tippet de Schnow on de Alpen, or in de darklin' efenin' ven de last rays on deir drementous heights seemet like *Wachfeuer* or Peacon-fires on dops of mighdy towers. *Ja*—he ging ober Feld und Thal—fieldt und dale, vale und dingle where de Dickets crow, slade und glade where rifulet waters flow, groves und rocky alcoves, mit deir shade—caverns and taverns—all mit shiftin' scenes—on all of vitch de awfool moundain-beaks look doun like magisdrates a vatchin' de communidy und seein' dot id pehave demselfs.

Und dere is druly, yosst ofer Innsbruck von of dese beaks vot hafe de ripudation to keep a vatch on dings in sheneral, und dis is die Frau Hütt,

Germany—Tyrol.

vitch is a shigontic mount crowned mit a vasd rock vitch has de shape of an *Amme*, or Noorse mit a shild in her lop. To pe sure id looks yoost ash moosh like an old man readin' a pook, or any ding else—de same as de face on Mont Blanc vot you sees from Geneva has a shdartlin' likeness to Hans Breitmann, or Dietrich of Bern or any oder crate man vot hafe a long peard—but dis is vot de Innsbruckers who bossessed de ardicle since forefer, say it is—und de Legende is ash follows:—

FRAU HÜTT.

Ere man's deets vere writ in shtory,
    Und vhile all vas wild und grand,
Denn die Shiants ruled in glorie,
    Ober all dis Alpen land,
Troo de Nord vere'er de Teuton
    Shbread abroad his mighdy soul;
Like de medeors, *Himmel* shootin'—
    Und deir *Hauptland* vas Tyrol!

Dey fited und dey drank hard,
    Und dey lived in roarin' sin,
Undil py and py dey conquered
    All de Valley of de Inn:
Dere vas joy among de winners,
    Und a sprec mit merry shouts;
Boot a-veepin 'mong de Inners,
    Ven dey found demselfs de Outs.

Now de Queen of dese wild victors,
    Vas benamed de Lady Hütt;
Und id seem from Legend's bictures
    She had peauty, grace und wit,
Mit de power of fastination,
    So dat afery hearts vas crackt,
Ven she coom dat operation
    Vot de Deutsch call *Zaubermacht.*

Und dere oopon dem moundain,
    She eruct a palace grand,
All oder piles surmountin'
    In dis fair Tyroler land;
Dere in wild luxuriation,
    Mit her lovers bold and free,
Dis crate Sovereign of de nation
    Lived in von dremendous spree.

Nefer carin' for de beoples,
    Mit deir sofferins und woe;
Any more dan Glocks in shdeeples
    Care for dings far down pelow.
Dose who nefer gare a copper,
    Lettin' veller-beins pass,
Dey some tay may come a cropper
    Over-het, und go to grass!

So it vas mit dis fair Riesin,
    Who mit all her witchery,
Only endet py disbleasin'
    Von who had more might dan she;

Germany—Tyrol.

Von dremendous on de Moral,
    In de Goot and Virduous line;
Und de endin' of deir squarrel,
    Vas he toorned her indo *Stein*.

All her lofers denn he hardens
    Indo crate dremendous blocks,
Und her lofely Rosen-gardens
    Shanged to tismal parren rocks;
Dere in shtone you see her sittin',
    Efer since de Long-ago,
Lookin' at de seasons flittin'
    O'er de valley doun pelow.

So de fleecy cloudts of mornin'
    Come a-sailin' o'er her het,
Und de *Abendroth* adornin',
    All its glorie round her shet;
But de Man ist gone forever
    Vot in early dimes she's known,
Like de foam-light on der rifer,
    Und her soul is toorned to shdone.

Boot dere is a sdrange relation
    Of dis Lady of de Hill,
Dot her anciend Fascinadion
    Is a lurkin' 'round her sdill;
For about her in de even,
    As from fairy-land remote;
Or ash chords yoost tropt from Heafen
    Lofely musik seems to floot.

Und aldough a petrifaction
  She is sdill a Lorelei;
Und it gifs her sodisfaction
  To enchant de basser-py,
Und he who hears dot chantin'
  Mit a *Zauber* spell is bound,
Und will nefer pe a wantin'
  To depard from Innsbruck town.

Vhile he singet dis Song dere came py an oldt Woman, apout four hundert yar oldt to yoodge py her looks, aldo she was carryin' a *Centner* or hundert veight of Sticks to sell in de town. So she shtop und listen to de Ballade und denn say:

" Dot is all fery fine, Vincenz—but dot is not de shtory ash I always heardt it."

"*Nun, Mutterche'*," say der Breitmann—"dake a trink, und let me hear your side of de gomplaint."

De oldt Frau opeyed orders—und unfoldet her legende as follow:

"Die Frau Hütt was a crate lady, dot might peen a baronesse, *Schau!* or a *Gräfin—gelt ja!*—und so proud ash a peagock und *herzlos*—ja—heartless as der teufel. Crate many beople is like dot, now—*Gott und die Mutter Gottes* hilf us all in our *Noth!*

"Von tay de Frau Hütt was ridin' on her horse vhen she met an *Arme*—a poor beggar voman. Dot peggar womans was a Witch. She peg Frau Hütt for a biece of Brod.

"De Frau Hütt had a shtein in her hand. She trow it ot de beggar-woman und *hit* her, und said, '*Friss du das du Aas!*' Eat dot you oldt Carrion!"

"Pff!—*im Nu*, war die Frau Hütt mit her horse all toorned into Stein. *Dort* sits she on the hill. But if any pody will climb oop on de Berg, he can hear at Twilight woonder-shine lofly Musick, mit Singen so fein as nefer was. Ja—peautiful—peautiful—peautiful—*alles sehr schön—Gelt, ja!*"

* * * *

"Der shendleman pears to pe a voreigner—*geltens!*" saidt der oldt Tyroler, mit a *Gems-bart* or a chamois-fedder in his hat, und a gostume, de brincipal ingredients of vitch seemet to pe gomposed of a cock-dail ofer de *Gems-bart*, and a punch of omelets to keep off de efil-eye or pring goot luck. Dese vere made of the teet' of a boar, a fox, a marmot, a crab's claw, a marten's upper jaw-pone, und de horns of a young chamois, all set in silber, mit a grün yacket, a broidered belt, und pare lecks mit braces.

"Der shendleman 'pears to be a voreigner," rebeat dis inderestin' object, "dough he talk Deutsch so goot ash I do. Boot dere is many men vot hafe a crate *Sprach-talent* for learnin' languashes."

"*Nun*," answer Hans, "id is drue I am von of dem vellers—for I can dalk Tyroler, Suabian, Bayerisch, Sächsisch, Allemannisch, Aargauer-Schwétzerisch, Platt-Deutsch und Pfälzisch, und dere to, Pennsylvanisch, mit a liddle Hoch-Deutsch. But as for mein *Heimath*, I was geporn in Schwaben, so you see ash I peen in America, I coomed a goot vay roundt to kit here."

"*Jao*," rebly der oldt Tyroler, "dot is like der Verwaller Görgli, vot go roundt by Venedig, to kit home acain mit some money. *Ja wohl!*"

Der Breitmann lisden to de dinklin far-away musick of de cow-bells ash it fall doun from de moudain-heighds five tousand feet apove indo de valley—und die disdant gry of de *Sennerinnen* or herd-girls, von to anoder, mit de roosh of a torrent ofer de grey rocks—und denn broduce from his shdores a pig flask of strong red wein.

"I kess," he saidt, "*mein Freund*—you vill kit de pest part of your shdory out of dis. Id's astonishin' how many tales und songs dis *Reiseflasche* of mine holts. *Nur zu! Trink, Kamarad!*"

Der oldt Tyroler dook a long und shdeady pull—a-pointin' de bottom of de flask at de soomit of de Solstein Alp—vitch is petween *acht* und nine tousand feet apove de level of ordinary minds. Denn he say:

"Der Görgli vas a man dot bastured his cottle in de Valley of de Verwall. Dere vas a *Brunnen* or shbring of goot fresh water vere he lofed to go to squench his durst. *Jao!*

"Vonce oopon a dimes in de hot of de tay he coomed to de shbring to kit some trink-wasser, und ash he sit dere he heardt a *Lärm* or noise a liddle vay off in *das Dickicht*, or dicket, und beep and see a most miseraplest, poorest liddle veller, all drippin' mit rags or *zerlumpt*, dot look fivefourt's shdarved to deat', a yoompin' oop mit afer so moosh droples, a-dryin' to kit some perries off a bush, to eat.

"'*Halt do und komm emol hier!*' say der Geörgl, 'if you vants someding to eat, you boor liddle out-hungered *Teufel.*'

"*Das Männlein* coom to him, und der Georgli gife him a goot pig biece of butter-bread—vitch *der Kleine* defhoured like he vas never seen foot before in all his life.—But vhen he cot done tone he say to Georgli :

"'*Du bist a gut* veller, und now I vill bay you for dot *Imbiss.*'

"'*Dank' schö, bin scho bezohlt*—I dank you, but I am paid alreaty,' rebly der Georgli. '*Sell is net unser Brauch,* dot is not our vashion to dake money for vot ve gife to a veller in gompany.'

"'*Ja,*' rebly der liddle mann, 'but ven I dells beoples to do somedings, dey shenerally opey me for deir own goot. You see de sand in dis brook?'

"'*Jao,*' said Georgli. 'Id is fery visiple ven I look ad id.'

"'Fery goot, Georgli,' rebly de liddle shap.

Germany—Tyrol.

'And if you will holdt your tongue und nefer say nodings to nopodies, you may coom to Luck mit it. Take so moosh of dat sand as you can corry in a sack, de more de petter for you—und trafel mit id to Venedig—or Venice.

"'Ven you kit dere, ashk for de palace of de Signore Moncenigo. Ven you go to de door und der Portier ashks you Vot you vant! You yoost rebly, "*Pronto.*" Denn you carry de Sand in und you will see vot you will pehold.'

"Tay by tay der Georgli gadder oop de sand, liddle py liddle, pecause dere only comed a liddle efery tay indo de blace, boot py und py he cot a *Sack-voll*, so much as he could bear, boot dot vas a goot deal.

"Denn he say nodings to nopody, boot go all alone mit himself to Venice. Dot vas *wondervoll* sights to see, as *schön* as nefer vas. So he ashk from a Tyroler vot he foundt selling braces und chamois-horns on der Marcus Plotz, vot he moost do to find der Signore Moncenigo.

"'*Potzblitz Landsmann*,' say der Tyroler-*bua*. 'Vot der Teufel hafe you cot to do mit so crate a lordt? *Nun, gut*—so kit indo von of dem

Gandolas vot you see, and der man will dake you dere—und *Glück sey mit Dir!*'

" Der Görgl go mit der Gandola und come to a fine palacet. He ashkt der Portier und say '*Pronto.*' Denn de Portier bow down to de ground, und gall some oder vellers, all tressed oop, und dey dake him troo many shblendit rooms, dill he coom to von vhere dere vas a crate tall Signore, vot look morally like a king. He sent de servants oot, und say :

"' *Willkomm* Georgli. I am clad to see you. Hofe you cot de Sand?'

" Der Signore Moncenigo look ad de Sand all ofer carefully—und denn say :

"' Georgl, here is a tousand ducats in gold for dot sand.'

" Der Georgl vas so glad ash he nefer vas. He dook de money, und der Signore say :

"' Tidn't you nefer see me pefore, Georgl?'

"' No,' reblied Georgl.

"' Look me in de face,' say der Signore.

"Und as Georgl lookt, der Signore shrunk oop shmaller und smaller, und his face wizened oop dill Georgli gry mit ashdonishment:

Germany—Tyrol.

"'*Gelt!* *du bist* der liddle old veller vot I gaved de butter-bread to.'

"'*Nun*, Georgl,' rebly der Signore—'you can holdt your tongue apout dot. Dere is dings in dis vorldt dot is pest not dalked apout in tescriptions.'

"Der Georgl redurned home, und bought him a *Schloss* und land, und pecame a crate man. But ven he hoonted to find de spring, he could not discofer brook nor sand nor anyding. Dot vos a mysdery too. Howefer de hint of der Signore Moncenigo vas enof to make him halt his tongue und nefer go pack to Italien.

"''Dwas all in Venice
   He gained his pennies:
Dot lofely city shwimmin in de sea,
   Und from dot menace
   He ne'er acain is
Redurned dot lofely city for to see.'"

Dere vas a *Silenz*—only proken py de monotone of de rooshing moundain torrent, und de far avay pleating of a goat. Der Breitmann lifd his eyes to Himmel und see in de plue farness a plack spot shwimmin troo de *Unendlich-keit* or mitout-end-ness of de summer sky.

"Dot," he said, "is an eacle, und he look, like a rich tourist, toun on all de blaces in de land, und tespise de boor goat vot always shday in von field."

"Goats can drafel too—somedimes," rebly der oldt Tyroler. "I know anoder legend, vot lets idself pe singed mit a tune, apout a *Ziegenbock* or goat, dot drafelled far und fast to distand lands."

"Dake anoder trink foorst," say der Breitmann. "Venefer you hafe de clock of a song, you petter wind id oop mit a bottle-key. *Dot ist so.*"

Dey held a silent tialogue of trinks, ven der oldt man open his sack, und dook oud a zittern, und *klimpered* mit his fingers oer de wires, und denn sang:

DE GOAT UND DE SHPOON.

 Dere is towrin', soarin' mountains
  In de lofty land Tirol,
 Dere is droopin', scoopin' valleys
  Into vitch de torrents roll;
 Eere is mighdy avalanches
  Vitch de icy giants flings
 In fight at one anoder,
  Dot roll like afery dings.

Germany — Tyrol.

In der Landestheir valley
   Lifed Simas Andra—he
Vent for a sommer season
   Afay to Hungary ;
Dere he maket a fine connection,
   For de volk dot knew him said
He live in fond affecdion
   Mit a wunder-lofely maid.

Boot ash peneat' de meadows
   A shinin' in de Sonn'
Dere ish deep und awful caferns
   Where cloomy coblins wone,
Or as tead men lie ge-buried
   All in a flowery dell,
Dere vas *vitchcraft* in de maiden
   Der Tyroler lofed so well.

Now ven de Autumn shattows
   Growed longer afery tay ;
Und all de crapes were vintaged
   Und de crops all poot afay,
Der Simas dell de *Mädchen*
   Vot lofe him heart und soul,
Dot he moost for de winter
   Go pack indo Tyrol.

De maiden she vas clefer—
   She make no row or fuss,
She know so vell dat nefer
   It pays to make a muss,

She said, " If you must go, dear,
    Oh blease retoorn und soon,"
Und gave him *zum Andenken*
    A wundrous silfer shpoon.

Ja wohl—dot shpoons vas curious
    Ash couldt pe, I'll pe pound,
I kess dot soosh anoder
    Vas novhere lyin' round,
Mit a *Teufel* on de handle
    A·sittin' in a tree ;
Und caracders upon id
    All fool of mysdery.

Nun, gut. Der young Tyroler
    Redurn unto his home ;
Not meanin' for de winter
    Some more aproad to roam,
Boot while to de enchandress
    His hearts remainet drue,
He likevise hat a *Mutter*
    Vot knowed a ding or dwo.

It coom on Christmas even,
    Ven afery von was glad ;
Und beoples pring togedder
    De finest dings dey had ;
Yoost dinkin' for disblayin'
    De time vas opportune,
Der Simas for a venture
    Brought oud his silfer shpoon.

Germany—Tyrol.

De gombany admired it,
    From hand to hand it poss'd;
Some say how fine de work vas,
    Some kessed how moosh it cost.
Dill it coom unto his *Mutter*,
    Who look at it amiss—
Denn ask him " Who *der Teufel*,
    Mein Sohn, have give you dis ?"

He dellt her pout de maiden
    He met vhere he did come,
Who gife de shpoon unto him :
    De Mutter answer " *Hum!*
Pefore you use dot *Löffel*,
    For fear of trick or sells,
I kess you'd petter try it
    A-feedin' some von else."

Dere vas a goat peside him,
    Its hair vas soft as silk,
Der Simas took der spoon up
    Und give dot goat some milk :
Soon as der goat hafe daste it,
    He tantz oopon der floor,
Denn bolted like der Teufel
    Right troo de open door !

Und rooshing madly onward,
    Dey saw dot he-goat go
Along de silent valley,
    In moonlight o'er de shnow.

De mutter say, "Dot Ziege
　Has cot to trafel far'n ;
He will not shtop his runnin
　Ondil he reach Hungarn."

Now when der Mai vas kommen
　Und leafs vere on de dree,
Und birds vere singin', Simas
　Vent pack to Hungary,
Led shdill py de affecdion
　Vitch in his soul he felt,
Dill he coom unto de housé
　Vhere dot lofely maiden dwelt.

Dere in a shady Garten,
　He found his lofely pride,
Emproiderin' a girtle—
　A goat vas py her side :
Der Simas bust oud laughin',
　Und she too, ven he say :
" Mine dear—aldough you spooned me
　I tidn't roon avay !"

Moràl. You've ofden heard it
　Und yet may hear it, soon.
You can win de heart's affection
　By gifin folk a spoon.
Vence coom de term of *spoonin*' :
　Boot dis ding you should notes,
Pestow dem on de sheepses
　Und nefer on de goats.

Germany—Tyrol.

Dere vas a silents for a pause, durin' vitch de two shmoked deir pipes, till der Breitmann said:

"You mendion dot dat hero vot to Venice went raisèd a Castel mit de results of his industrie. He buildt his house oopon de Sand—dot vas a pad foundations."

"*Nè*," rebly der Tyroler—"it tepends on vot kind of sand you use. Gold sand maket a fery goot *Grund* for a house. Peobles say ven land is all sand und moss id is goot for noding. But Moss ist wort' money somedimes."

"*Ja*," answer Hans. "In de Yiddish language *moes* or *moos* means money."

"Und I knowed of a man," respondet der Tyroler, "dot got rich mit Moss. Dot vas a long dime ago. Dis veller had peen a robber vot pelonget to de band of Schinderhannes, der Räuber of der Rhine. *Ja wohl*. *Nun*, ven der band vas gebrochen oop und Schinderhannes vas *gerädert* or vheeled off, dis Deutscher infentet a new way to make a livin'. *Ja wohl*. He vent into de forest-woods und filled a great sack mit Moss.

"Denn he vent do a *Gast*-house, or tavern, und ashk for der pest bett-room. *In der Nacht* he rosed und gerippt oop de fedder-bett und shtoled all de fedders und put dem mit demselfs indo de sack, und de moss he used to stoff de *Bett* mit. Denn he do it all oop acain mit a sew-needle und tread, so goot ash efer was."

"Nun dot was fery *sinnreich*—und clefer!"

"*Nicht wahr?* *Nun, gut,* he nex' tay he go way mit de fedders und carry dem home vhere he sell fedder-betts mit a shop. *Ja so.* Und he garry dis pisiness on for fifdeen yar mit aller-greatest securidy, pecause beoples tid not dis cofer for long dimes dot de fedders was moos, und denn dey dinked id vos der bett-seller vot schwindled dem.

"Nun, vonce oopon a dimes he coom to a *Gasthaus* vhere he hot shdole fedders long pefore, und forgot it. Dis dimes, hafin no moos he had *gestohlen* some hay und shtoff his sack mit id. Now he left der sack a lyin' unadvertendly on de grund, und dere come py an shack-ass vot shmelt de fodder, und tore der sack open und pegan to eat de hay, und der *Gastwirth*, dot

Germany—Tyrol.

is der landlord, observe dis, und mistrow, or sospecdt somedings—ven all at vonce de fedders flash oopon his memory—und he say, '*Potzblitz!* dis must pe der *Sakermentskerl* vot shteal das *Gefieder*, or de plumage out of mine betts! *Wart nur, du infamer verruchter Schlingel—ich bring Dir eins!* Yoost wait you invamous accursed mishcreants, und see vot you'll catch! *Dir wird 'was schönes gebacka, du verdammter Teufelssohn! Hol dich der Henker, du Frankfurter Aas!*'—mit efer so many more Dutch cuss-words, for he was so angry dot he dalk *Deutsch gradaus*.

"So dot night dey set a votch troo a keyholes—und vot you dinks dey see mit demselfs—

'All in de finster Mitternacht
Ven honest volk in shleeps vere lockt,'

put dis *Galgenbube* a rippen open de *Bett*, und confisticatin' de fedders! So dey roosh in oopon him, und schlog him on de kop, und boot him mit kicks, und tie him mit a rope und stick him on prison—vhere he gonfess all his grimes. *Ja wohl*. Mein Grossvater hafe seen his kop—dot is his het—many a yar ober de City-gate—und vot vas woondervoll—de *Raben* or ravens shtick it full mit fedders, as a cushion mit stick-needles. *Ja wohl !* "

Und here I gannot refrain from be-markin' dot accordin' to der learned Schlachtenschlagerius in his Buch, *De Plumis Arripiendis*, Nuremberg, 1530. die Idee of dis Tale is far more antiquateder dan de peginning of dis century. Dis wrider draces it pack, *foost* to a Classic source, dot vas der Shackdau in Esops *Fabulæ* vot shtealed de beacock-fedders, himself to ornamente ; *Segondly* to de primaeval German-Teutonic Frau Holle, who is de goddess of Fedders vitch ash she ist an infernal deity imblies shdealin. Derefore ven it shnows, de Dootch shildrens say dot " de *Federsack* or fedder-pag, of Frau Holle is borsted open," or dat " Frau Holle is makin' de Fedders fly." Now dis Frau Holle ist Frigga or Freya, for vitch reason I peliefe dot in dis shtory, apout der feller's shtealin fedders, we hafe de relics or draces of a myth based oopon de oldt Northern worship of dis goddess. Dot's *so.*

CHAPTER VI.

VY DE ALL-ALONELINESS OF NATUR MIT SPOOKS AND OFER-NATURAL PEINS GEFILLED IS. DE BALLAD-SHTORIES OF DE KAUNSER-WITCH — DE HAZEL-WITCH — DIE BELL OF KALTEIN UND DIE WOONDERFULL PEASE.

" Truly there can be no doubt, as Gregorius relates (Lib. 3, Dialogorum c. 7) of Bishop Andrew, that demons and all kinds of strange beings dwell in lonely places, uninhabited by man. For it befell to him by night that he *solitudinis pavore turbatus*, frightened by Solitude, suddenly beheld a vast assembly of malignant Spirits."—*Tractatus de Confessionibus Maleficorum et Sagarum.* Auctore PETRO BINSFELDIO, A.D. 1596.

VEN a man is in de dremendous scenerie of Mountain-Natur where all is silentz proke at intervales py strange ooncanny sounds like ravens' grys, de wailin' of die Winds—de fall of

Hans Breitmann in

rocks—de Torrent flowin' like an entless Voice—while far above forests on forests rise like cloudts apove de cloudts dill lossed in light, denn he veels dot Solitude is almost von mit Sooplimity. *Und noch weiter* dot is, furder shtill, vhen he see, as is fery gommon in de Tyrol, so many cliffs und beetlin' risin rocks like towers, turreted, and castles old, windowed und gated ash by ancient art, so like to *machicoles* or crenelles, seeming more like dem in de *Abendgluth* or rosy efenin—den Solitute mit such helps, itself *einflüstert* or whisper into oos dot dere is Dings dot live here—dings not of Eart', spiridual und wild—und dot it spooks und ghosts vhere Man's pegone!

Ja wohl—as in de oldten dime de magination of de Geisterseher beoplet de *Wüste* or Wildernesses of Syria und Egypten mit all kinds of Lemures, Daemons und consimilar Operations soosh as Satyrs und Fauns,—so der dweller in de mountains high, seems raiset mit height unto Supernal dings, und efer dinks on spectral Elvish life. De English tourist may miss it, efen if he drafel efer so teeply indo de

Germany—Tyrol.

Tyrol, but a Sud-Deutscher dot is in touch, or in *Berührung* or *Empfindung* mit de beoples, will soon find dot dere is apout so many Spooks, or *Butze* in de in-land, avay from de towns ash dere is in-dwellers or onhapitans. Dus to example dey pelieve dot ven de *Sennerleut'* or folk dot take care of de gattle, soosh ash cows mit bools, und maken milk und butter on de *Alm'* or mountain meadows, all pelieve dot vhen dey mofe oud of deir huts in de Autumn, de Spooks all dake deir blace und wone in dem all de Winter. Upd dese ghostly In-dwellers is of apout sixdy tifferent kinds, de brincipal bein' de *Geists* or ghostes und ghostesses of *Sennerleut'* or cow-herds vot gommitted some grimes soosh ash losin' gattle und not accountin' for dem to de owners; derfore dey moost live in timid misery till dey are *erlöset* or set free py somepody who fery ofden becomes a treasure of Gold by so-doin. De numper of Legende vot prove dis is beyont all pelief, derefore it follow dot dere moost pe some *Wahrheit* or Trut' in it. *Ja wohl.*

Zweitens or Secontly. Dere is tausents of

Hexen or Witches dot haunt or spook in dese blaces. Und dis remind me dot ven I vas in Kauns, dere was an oldt woman dat told me dis Story as follow, from which I maket dis Song:

THE KAUNSER-WITCH.

List und I'll sing you a sing-u-lar tale,
Dere lived in old dimes in de Kaunser-dale
In a haus dot is shtandin' efen now,
A man dot had a peautiful *Frau*,
Und a gleferer womans—oopon my soul!
Vas not to be fount in all de Tyrol.
Yet mit so many strange and mysderious vays,
Dot Nopody givet her oonmingelt braise;
Und efen her Mann was always in doubt
As to somedings in her he couldn't make out;
A ding vitch we know—don't very well go,
For dough it may charm on a virst acquaindance,
'Dis cerdain to lead in de end to repéntance.

Now dis Mann was py trade a shoemakér,
Und it happend von efenin he saidt to her:
" I would like to go to-morrow morn
Indo mine fieldt to harvest mine corn;
It is ripe you know, und alreaty cut,
Und dere it lies for the gadderin'—but
I hafe work in de haus—und dot is drue,
Und I'm dropled not knowin' yoost vot I most do,
For if rain should fall it would be forlorn,
Since dot wouldt cerdainly shpoil mein Corn."

Germany—Tyrol.

So he spoked his wife. *Darauf* set she,
" *Ach, geh' nur!*—yoost leaf dot harfest to me,
All of de matter in order I prings,
If you leaf me alone like averydings."
" How will you do it?" " Yoost nefer you mind,
In de efenin all will pe ready you'll find;
Go to your vork like a nice liddle Mann,
Und I'll manage de harfest so goot ash I can."

Now when dese worts to der Mann were saidt,
All kind of dinkin coom indo his headt,
Und all de next tay it roon in his kop,
How der *Teufel* his wife would harfest de crop;
Dill he say to himself: " No harm I'll cotch
If I hides mineself in de wood to watch:
I don't like dings mysderious so;
Vot die Frau is a-doin' der Mann should know.
To catch a goblin you take an elf."
So he vent py night und conceal't himself,
Oop in a tree all tuckered avay.
Where he saw de corn in de *Acker* dot lay.

At mitternight as he lay conceal'd,
His Frau com' glidin' into de field,
Holdin' a proom like fire in her hand
Which she wafe like a queen when she give command;
She look at the corn in many a row,
Und all dot she say was, " Blow, Wind—blow!"

Vhen yoost in de momendt dot she shpoke,
A derriple wind like a shtorm awoke,
Und de wind it tid votefer she pid,
For it lifted the roof of his barn like a lid
Vhen you raise de top of a *Kist* or box,
Or open a toor to a berson dot knocks ;
Mein Gott ! 'Dwas a derrible sights to see
How de dings was manag'd py Sorcery !

Den it lifted all of de Shocks of corn,
Und garry dem vlyin indo de barn ;
Hei how dey flittet und ho ! how dey flew !
It all was tone in a minute or two,
Ja—in a momendt id all was o'er,
Und die roof of de barn shut down as before.

Die Frau was to-haus vhen der Mann com' in,
She say to her huspand—" Vhere hafe you peen ? '
" I hafe peen Gott knows in dis life of mine
Full many a time in trouple und *Pein*,
Many a dime in sorrow und smart,
But noding pefore efer vent to my heart,
Noding e'er grieved me—I dells you true,
Like vot dis night I hafe seen you do."

She borst out laughin' und saidt mit shkorn :
" Dot is my dank for safin' your corn
Dot hat else peen spoiledt mit rain und frost : "
He answer, " I'd rat'er id all were lost,

Germany—Tyrol.

All dot I hafe in de worlt I'd miss,
Rat'er dan have it be-safed like dis;
Der Teufel is nefer a trusty friendt,
Und all petween us is now at an end;
I lofed you vonce—put it all is o'er,
Go vhere you will. We shall meet no more."

Mit ringing laughter she filled de room,
Und leapt' mit a shout on her fiery broom,
"Goot py denn, my *Narr*, if you like," say she;
"Fire mit water can nefer agree,
De witch is a fool who weds mit a man
Dot wont dake money whenefer he can,
Und der Mann anoder who marries a witch
Und like to pe poor vhen he mighdt pe rich:
Oben, hinaus und nirgends an,
Whoop in de mitnight, I'll fly when I can—
Goot py for efer mine goot liddle man!
Goot py to you mit your corn und your house,
I'm off to de Brocken—*heraus! heraus!*"

Off she shot in de silent night,
Far in de tistands he watched de light,
As it dimmed away, of de fiery broom,
Denn he heav't a sigh in de darkenet room.
Was he griev't or not? *Ach*, who can tell?
De brisoner sighs ven he leaves his cell!

"Nun," saidt Breitmann, "vhedder dere is Witcheses dot can ride on prooms und raise de

Wind in a Shtorm, *buchstäblich*, or literally makin' a tevil of a litter of dings, is more dan I can be-dear or schwear at. But dot dere is womens who are so mysteriös und fool of eggcentric hidden caprices, und unsteady habits und wanton idle wills mixed oop with cleverness und gootness, as to pe really soupernatural, is *drue*—und whet'er dey have sold demselfs to der Teufel or not—dey are *dere*—dot is dey are out of humanity und Natur. Denn again dere are many, or all, of dese, who for some liddle wrongs pecome so outerorderly findictive und shpiteful, follerin' oop Revenge mit all deir soul und life, dot a white Christian can-not really oonderstand dem at all—so id is no crate vonder dot he dinks dey are all de sisders und shildren of Satan."

"Dot is drue," remarked his frient der Professor. " Und yoost ash dere is a certain relict of de oldt savage or giant, of early dimes, in efery man, so is dere a drace of de witch in de pest und sweedest of women—or a lofe of suffering vhen it is caused py *herself*, vitch flatters vanity —und vhere you find *dot*, dere is de plack hellwitch, und de dree trops of Teufel's blood—

seldom a-wantin' in de fairest pody. Nor does Religion take it oud of dem, pecause de piousest nuns, und Presbyterianest Scotchesses, und New Englandest proprietesses, und Moralistes, alvays seem to me to pe de unforgivinest und spite fullest of all de Witches, at heart. *Nun, gut—* we are all boor wretches—Gott forgife oos ! "

"Vot de spitefoolness und *Teufelslust* of witches concerns," say der Schoolmaster ash he lift *der Deckel* off his *Biermaas* und *sauft* a long trink— "*D'rauf kann ich was erzähle*—on dot I can dell a shtories." Und mitout waitin' to pe squeezed —boot foorst profidin' himself mit anoder goot pull at de moog ash *Viaticum* for his journey, he rooshed onvarts in his plind career as be- vollows :

DE HAZEL WITCH.

Nort' of Botzen on a hill,
Shtands a grey und time-worn tower
Marred by many a winter's chill
Summer's sun und Audumn shower,
Shtandin' high und broud und lone
Like a grim lord vot shbeak to none,
Least of all to men ven he
Is in old age mit poferty.

Hans Breitmann in

Wondrous dings dot Tower has seen
In de oldten dime I ween,
For dwas pilt ash all men know,
Full a tausent Yar ago,
'Twas a Wälsche magian
Who de structur' foost pegan,
Murmuring de tree-fold shpell
He pringed to him de fiends of hell:
Denn a maiden foorst of all
Dey build' alive into de wall,
Dot her spirit, ash dey say,
Mighdt guard *der Thurm*, und well, for Aye.
Py demon skill de whole was made,
Py demon hands dose walls were laid,
Und teufels carved de forms grotesque,
Ofer each arch in wild burlesque,
So dot when finish't from dot hour
Id was well call'd der Defil's Tower.

    Ages hafe vlown
      Boot de Tower still
    Grey und alone
      Shtands on de hill,
Ever uncanny its castellany
With imps in every gorner und cranny,
    Und for its masters
      Dose lords of disasders;
    Wizards or Sorcerers
      Pringin, of course, terrors,
Raisin of Sturms mit *Hagel und Blitz*
A-shkarin de beoples all rount indo vits.

Germany—Tyrol.

So it vent for many a yar
Und der Teufel was alvays dere,
Dill id com' to bass in de Anno Domini
Sefenteen hundert mit fifty six
Dot an oldt vitch mit sin und ignóminy
All in dot Tower was blayin' her dricks,
Doin' her tamtest de beasants to vex
Und was generally known ash *die Haselhex*'
    Or de Hazel-witch
    Cause she garry a switch,
Or a rod dot vas coot from a hazel-dree,
De gauses of vitch you shall bresently see.

Dis *Hazelhex*' had an orphan yout'
Whom she kepdt I peliefe in trut'
    As a Teufelshex',
    Only to vex
Dease und torture, pe-devil und spite,
Worry und hurry from morn to nighdt,
Vhen he was goot she kickt him aroun'
Und vhen he vasnt, ge-knockt him down,
Und shmack his vace—und treatet him—yes,
Like a canni-bally old Sorceress!

Von efenin in Autumn dis witch, saidt she
To her poy, " Now come mit your pasket mit me,
    Id is dime to run
You lazy, itle idiots-son!
   You tont want no more rest,
   So com' to de forest,

Hans Breitmann in

Und gadder nuts, you undershtood—
Vhile I go furder into de wood
Vhere I have cot somedings for to do.
Boot mind dis dings vot I say to you :
    If you dare—
    Pe-ware ! pe-ware !
If you dare to follow me
Und be-seeket any dings for to see,
Py shingo !—I'll make minsch-meat of dee,
    Und dot is true,
    Uh-hu ! Uh-hu ! "
She lookt like der Teufel ash she said it,
Und he put it toun to der Teufel's credit.

Soon dey coom to de forest ground
Vhere de Nuts vere a lyin' all around,
Put de poy he took em mit sorryfool feelin',
Pecause a-dakin dese noots vas shtealin',
Und he knew dot if caught py de owner a doin-it,
He vouldt fery cerdainly soon be rue-in it.
Und ash he pickt he kep' dinkin' und dinkin'
Into vot blace de oldt witch could pe slinkin',
    Und vot de gause
    Of dis secresy vas ;
Dill at last he say, " May der Teufel swallow her !
Anyhow I am goin' to follow her ! "

    Saidt und done,
    Away he run,
Trackin' her closely on her path,
Nefer a-heedin' her spite or wrath,

Germany—Tyrol.

Dill he come to a blace in a lonely wold !
Und oh !—vot dings he vas dere pehold !
Five hundert witches und seventy dree,
All on a howlin' und derriple spree !
    Roundt on a dree
Hung a hundert skulls in which shone a light
Green und red from de eyes so pright,
Ofer dem all in de gadderin night,
Vot made a remarkaply derrible sighdt ;
    Und on a crate shtone,
    Mit vines o'ergrown,
Sat a forty-teufel orchestrá
Dot on forty instrumends tid blay
To de witches und wizzers a yellin' und tantzin',
Huggin' und shkreeming and leapin' und prancin'.

Soon ash de witch appear'd on de cround,
Dere vas von crate gry from de rest around,
Und von of dem saidt, " You're de last of all
Who hafe come to-night to tantz at de ball ;
Derefore you moost pe torn to bieces,
Ash at gander-pullins de men tear geeses ;
Dot is de law mitout a doubt,
Und ve are a goin' to garry it out.
Mit a *Hup, hurrah ! Potz Teufel und Blitz !*
Dey flew at de *Hexe* und tore her to bits,
Und trowed dem here—und scattert dem dere,
So de bieces were vlyin' apout in de air.

At last ven weary of kissin' und fightin',
Tantzing und trinkin', und yellin' und bitin',

Dey gaddered de bieces of deir victim;
Und vhen from here und dere dey had pick'd 'em,
Und laid in order the mangled vitch,
Dey stroked de whole mit a *hazel-switch*,
Solemnly sayin': "*Abuscabornio*
Aldiboronti phoscophornio,
Chrononthologos—Bambochides
Adenocluninstaridysarchides
Appalecheosmoccommetico,
Barago bango ballabamdetico!"
    Vhen at de word,
    Soon as she heard
De sound of dese magical rhymes so clefer,
De vitch yoomped as lively ash efer;
Und denn unto her de oders said:
"We hafe refived you from de dead,
Und now you may live mitout pain or stitch,
Till some one shall call you a *Hazel-Witch;*
Pe it in earnest or pe it in fun,
You will denn fall tead as sure as a gun."

Hid, und to keep his silentz still able,
De poy had listen'd to afery syll-aple;
Havin' a mind apofe his stadion,
He efen rememperd de tinpancation,
Und bored in his memory de liddle switch,
Und tidn't forget de "*Hazel-Witch.*"
"Und now I hafe cot der Teufel's elixir,
Nex' dime she's sassy," said he, "I'll fix her!"

Nor tid he have fery long to wait,
For oop she com' mit a hurryin' gate,
Und look in his pasket und gry, "*Potzbutz!*
Du Galgenbube—vhere ish de nuts?
Du Aas—du Esel—du Luder Heinz!
Wart nur du Schlingel! Ich bring dir Eins!"
Und she *schlog* him like *Blitzen* on de kop,
Und hit like she nefer was goin' to shtop ;
So he soon moost hafe passed from dis Werlt to de nex',
If he hadn't hollered : "*Du Haselhex'!*"

    De word ge-spoken,
    De charm ge-brocken,
    De *Zauberspruch* said ;
    She lay mit de tead,
    De form py dunder!
    All tumpled asunder.
De het was here und de lecks were dere,
In a scatteration eferywhere,
Und I really cannot plame de poy
Dat he tantzted around de collection mit yoy.

Shtill you may see dot casdle fair
So rosy-red in the sunset air ;
Boot cofered mit ivy and grey old moss,
For dings ain't now like dey used to vas,
For vitches no longer circle on high,
Und swoop on deir prooms from de mitternight sky

Und imps no longer mit gry und yell,
Seem pent on raisin' barticolar Höll',
As if by Meister Lucifer led,
Dey were pizzy mit paintin' de settlement red;
For now ash we know der Teufel is dead,
Yed shtill de pheasants mit dremplin tone,
Will shpeak of de tays dot is passt und gone —
Dose derriple dimes of oldt in which
Das Land was ruled by de Hazel Witch.

"*Ja*," bemark der Professor. " Dere is somedings fery mysteriös apout Hazels. In de old German poetry, dot push is alvays ge-called Frau Hazel—like it hat a soul—und vherefer dis occurs to a plant or bird it means dot it is regardet ash a supernatural pein'—likevise has it a crate moral influence—being generally used to vip liddle pad poys mit. Und dere is ofden fount some Hazel nuts in ancient graves as a sympol—pecause yoost like a putterfly hide herself in a goccoon, to coom vlying out like averydings—or de nut-kernel hide in de shell pefore it boorst upwards into a plant—so de humane soul itself in de ground hide must ere it rise to eternal day-life. Derefore is it lucky nuts of any kind in de bocket to carry, ash I

Germany—Tyrol.

mineself horse-shestnuts agains' de rheumatism do bear. But shpeakin' of Witches in de Tyrol, I know anoder tale which ven it gepleasin' is de honourable companie to, I vill here norate."

Und he norated as follow :

DE BELL OF KALTERN.

    Oh de shoorsh-pells at even,
      How shweetly dey ring !
    Like angels in heafen
      Dey murmur und sing !
    Where musik can trafel,
      Deir echoes are found ;
    Und naught dot is efil
      Can list to de sound.
So softly, so quaintly dey chime in deir blay,
So gently, so vaintly denn dyin' afay—
    Fading out—mit de tay !

Now no witch can hang out vhere de Church *Glocke* hang,
For pein' ge-blest dey're ofraidt of de clang ;
At de fery foorst sound of soosh pells dey are lost,
Und shrivel like skeeters vhen hit py a frost,
Und ter Teufel himself vouldt pe off on de wing
Vhen de crate pell of Kaltern pegan for to ring,
Ei ! dot busted oop, like a sight for to see,
In grand scatteration, die whole gompanie,

Und goot Christians like oos arn't more vritenet of Höll'
Dan de vitches vere shkeered at de sound of dot pell!
    Oontil at de last,
    Deir patience all past,
Und de fery end thread of the skein pein spun,
Dey shwore dere must cerdainly Somedings pe done;
Und Somedings dey tid too, at once, dot is "poz,"
Und you soon will soormise vot de handiwork was.

    Dhere's a widow in Eppan
      Mit glance like a dart,
    A derriple veapon
      Vot bierce efery heart,
    Mit de sofdest of laughder,
      De schweetest of shmiles;
    Gott knows vot com' after
      Vhen vonce she peguiles!
    Und dis lady of Eppan
      Is charmingly dresst;
    She feedeth on capon,
      Mit wein of de pest:
Dough vhence she derivet de food und de clo'se,
Und how she got dese dings, or com' to have dose,
Is vot she hafe nefer to no von disclose,
Vitch maket moosh woonder—ash you may suppose.

Now ven beoples pefore dem keeps alvays a curtain,
Dere's somedings pehind it unright, dot is cerdain;
Und all vere assur't dot dis peautifool widow
Hung out vot de French call a fery large *rideau*.

Germany—Tyrol.

    But Hermann von Valk,
      A shivalric yung plade,
    Who vas not of talk
      Nor of myst'ries afraid,
    Vas all de more taken,
    Enshanted und shaken,
    Enroptured und smashed,
    Be-glamoured und mashed
Py de peautiful eyes und die wunderfoll mystery
Dot seem to enfelope dis Lamia's hisdory;
Und von tay vhen in shport de fair wittow would task him,
He schwored he would do her votefer she ask him,
He gare not a shdraw were it dot, were it dis—
If she only wouldt gife him von ropturous giss.

    Mit de winsomest shmile
    Dot wouldt fetch you a mile,
    Und a Soft in her voice
    Dot would gife you no choice
Boot to do vot she vanted: "*Geliebter*," say she,
"I can only ask someding shivalric from dee,
Soosh ash nople und gallant young vellers perform
Vhen deir hets dey are prafe, und deir hearts dey are warm;
    Yet dot vot I want
    You can easily crant.
In vact 'tis as easy as yompin' a hurdle,
Yoost glimp de church-sdeeple a bearin' dis girdle;

De shdeeple of Kaltern,
  You know id fool well ;
Und binding, you shall turn
  Dis belt round de pell ;
    Bind it und wind it,
    Und vhen you have twined it—
Vhen dis is done und my love ist returnet—he
May giss if he like to de ent of Eternity."

  Now as you may hafe guessed,
    Dis yung Hermann von Valk
  Vas not, truly confesset,
    A man easy to balk ;
So as soon ash de widow her yarn had spun,
He yoomp to his feets, und gry eagerly '*Done!*
For soosh a revart I geschwear py mein' Soul,
I'd belt all de bells in das land of Tyrol !
Gife me de girtel. I dells you vot,
I'll pe pack dis efenin "—Und off he shot.

    Now dough dis Hermann
      Hot no scrupulosity,
    Yet as a German
      He'd crate curiosity ;
Vitch ding is de Mutter of all suspicion ;
So he toorn it ofer mit more precision,
Und he say to himself, " I vish I could tell
Vot it is dat she want of a-beltin' de bell ?
'Tis fery mysteriös—*hum!*—let me see !
Soopose I virst try it oopon dis tree ;
Dere's noting at all in de vay to prefent
Soosh a liddle hormless exsperiment."

Germany—Tyrol.

So half-oondinkin', or half in yoke,
He pound der Girtle apout an oak;
It was a most trementous dree,
Biggerer nopody efer tid see
Shtandin' alone so grand und solemn,
Mit drunk ash dall und ash shtrait ash a column;
But shkarce dot girtle was brought around,
Und shkarce der belt on de park was pound,
Ven a crash like a tausent Donners came
Und pefore his eyes all swum in a flame,
Ash if hell had proke loose in fery fact,
Und from dop to pottom de oak-tree crack'd
Und de fragments flew afar und wide,
Vhile der Herr von Valk lay stunn'd 'long side.

De bells were a-ringin'—mitnight—twelf'
Pefore der yung gentleman coom to himself,
Und when he cot dere—" Potz-blitz!" said he,
" I am clad dot I tried de belt on a tree,
For if I had bound it round de bell
Vitch de witches all fear like poison und Höll "—

* * * * * *

Vhen havin' saidt dis he soodenly stop'd,
Ash if an *idée* on his senses had dropp'd,
Und he roar'd "*Donnerhagel mit Blitz und* pitch!
Now may I pe tam—but de widow's a—witch!
Es leuchtet mir ein—I pehold it clear!
Ash I see yon Moon in her silber sphere:
Dot vas a nice liddle task dot the vidder

Gave me to do, vhen I coom to consider.
Subbose inshteat of a dree I had blaced
Dot peautiful Girtle apout mine waist!
Dot wär an elegant shange of scene,
Hol sie der Teufel!—Vhere vouldt I peen?
So sure ash a Böhm trinks *Slibovitz*,
Bust to bieces und plown to bits :
So now I will go mit mine self to Haus'
Schöne Hexe! Mit dir ist's aus!
I can shtand a crate deal," he said mit a sigh,
"But not der *Teufel*—und so—good-pye!
Py dis atfenture I plainly see
Dot two of a trade can nefer agree :
Ven von has tolled de oder can't 'tell.'
Und a belle, if a witch, is afraid of a Bell."

"*Sehr gelungen,*" remark der *Schulmeister*. "Well tone. De reason vy witches cannot pear to hear church-bells ring is dis—dot mit efery shtroke ven dey ring de *Hexe* must her breat' in-hold, till de sound dies away—so dot if der Sexdon ring fery strong und long dey kits 'most to deat' choke-strangled—worser as when you yourselfs burnin' Sulphur in-breathe. Ja, dot is drue! Now de Vitches lofe to make Sturms mit Donner und Blitz—und for dis dey in de cloudts ride, de crops to destroy

Germany—Tyrol.

—ash is vell pe-known. And of dot I mine-
Self do a ballad know——"

"Sing it," gry de gompany.

So he sang:

DE WUNDERFOLL PEASE.

   Karl der Studènt
    Was dot kind of a Mann
     Vherefer he vent
      He learn all dot he can;
He hat kenned de Wälschers in Italy,
Und dravelled in Deutschland dings to see.
So gar among de Frenchers in France;
Vhere was somedings to learn he ne'er lossed a chance.
    Vherever he go
     Or vherefer he wander'd,
    On earth pelow
     His time vas ne'er squandered,
Und derefore in time ash his industrie meritet,
He got to pe fery excessifely er-u-dite.

    One day in Lavérn
     Near de town of La Roche,
    He sot in a tavern
     A-waitin' de coach,
Und foundt an old *Buch*. Says he, " Dere's a minute
I'll yoost dake a look und see vot may pe in it;"
'Tvas a werk on Magic and Divination,
Und in he read dis Incantation:

Hans Breitmann in

> "*Take a human skull*
> *And let it pe full*
> *Of church-yart earf,*
> *Und next in dot dirt*
> *Tree peas dou must sow,*
> *Und denn let 'em grow*
> *Till anoder crop*
> *Shbrings out of de Kop;*
> *Und denn, if you blease,*
> *Pick all of de Peas,*
> *Und next, mit regard,*
> *Keep 'em all till dey're hard,*
> *Und denn—to see fun—*
> *Load 'em into a gun,*
> *Und fire dem off, oop into de sky,*
> *But look out vhen you shoot dot you aim de gun high.*"

Karl hadn't no dime to read any more,
Vhen de coach com' a rottlin' oop at de door;
So he drafelled avay— boot dot charm vot he read,
Somehow would nefer go out of his head;
Nor de gurious manner in vitch he come by it,
Dill von tay he shwore, "*Donnerwetter*, I'll try it!
Vhet'er der teufel pe in it or not.
I would like yoost to see vot'll coom of de shot."
So he got an old skull, *secundum artem*.
Und in it he blanted de peas to start 'em,
Und dey shprouted undoubted so frisch und fine,
Und growed to a fery mocknificent vine,

Germany—Tyrol.

Ash all dings grow from churchyard sods,
Till dere hung from it many well-ripen't pods ;
Und vhen dey were hard peyond a doubt,
Der Student gaddered und shelled dem out,
Und he note mit amaze vhen he come to pull it,
Dot avery one vas ash hard as a bullet.

      Dus having pegun,
      He dook an old gun,
Ash quaint a *Bix* ash you efer did see,
      Datet M.D.C. . . .
Inlaidt mit silfer und ivory,
      Mit a curious lock,
      Und an epony shtock
On which was inlaid—und dis is de trut' :
Domine dirige—" *Lord help me shoot !* "
Ven hafin' charged it mit excellent powder,
Proceedet mit paper and peas to crowd her,
You'd hafe dinked dot he wouldt have himself exploded,
Mit haste so impatient—*nun, gut*—'tvas loaded.

      Now yoost at dot minute,
      Like teufels were in it—
A dunderin', thunderin', derriple shtorm
Came boorstin' apout, all ofer de farm,
Enof to greate a trementous alarm,
      Mit drees doun crashin',
      Und blitzen a-vlashin',

De wind a roaring mit terriple sound,
Und der fery old teufel to pay all round,
Vhile yoost oferhet in fisible sight
Came a Cloud—ash gloomy and dark as Night;
Dere vas Somedings in it so vild und grimm
Dot look yoost ash if it were comin' for Him!
Like a Dragon dot vouldt—if it had de apility—
Go for him smack mit de ootmost hostility,
Und aldough soosh a veelin most cerdainly damnin' is
It woke in der Student a *gaudium certaminis*
When you swear you "don't care if te foe can lick ten o' me,
Gife me a shanse und I'll fly at de enemy."
Und so dis redoubtaple *Musen-sohn*,
Mit an *Ave Maria*, put oop his gun,
Und remem'brin' vot de *Buch* told him he should,
Aimed his parrel ash high as ever he could;
Porpendicular unto de shky,
At de cloud's mittel he denn let vly;
   Slap he sent her
   Right into de centre;
Und nefer on earth vas a gun dot rung
Mit soosh a trementous und horrible "BOONG!"
It vas hearet, I shwears you oopon my soul!
All de way ofer de whole Tirol!

   Boot oh—vot horrors!
   Ven doun from de shky
   Somedings—not porous—
   Seemed for to vly,

Germany—Tyrol.

Somedings solid—mitout jocosity—
Coomed shootin' to eart' mit de ootmosd felocity !
Id fell peside him—yoost on de shpot—
Oont it vas—a human peings—*bei Gott!*
   A female corpus—
   Nod von dings or todder—
   A ding amorpus
   Vot maket him—shooder !
Id seemet his plood to ice to convert,
Vhen he saw'd dis Horror coom shootin' downvart !

Ja wohl, ja wohl, ja wohl, ja wohl!
A womans trest in a black *Camisol*,
A shpecies of woollen garment ; which is
Especially worn py feminine vitches
   Vhen dey ride in a shtorm,
   Pecause id is warm ;
So aldough id serfes fery well to protect her,
Id is also known as a vitch detector.

Denn soon all de beoples gaddered around
To look at de corpse lyin' dere on de ground ;
Till von saidt : " I know her—upon my soul !
'Dis de vickedest Vitch in all Tirol !
   Deres isn't a Hex'
   Of all de sex,
Nor a *Teufelskind* of de Compagnie,
Dot has made so moosh droples or efils as she ;
None of dem all so horrid or *grob* is,
Ave Maria—ora pro nobis !

Hans Breitmann in Germany—Tyrol.

Dis is de shtory. Id all is o'er,
But Karl nefer vent on such hoonting no more ;
Yet dis ding for a Moral he learned py de py :
*Vhen you go for pig game always aim your gun
   high!*

CHAPTER VII.

A SHTORY FROM BOTZEN—DE DEAD HEAD VOT MAKE DE FORTUNE OF DER STUDENT JOHANNES.

"Circa annum Domini 1200 in Vienna repertum fuit Caput cujusdam defuncti, lingua ad huc integra, cum labiis, et loquebatur recte. Episcopō autem interrogante, qualis fuisset in vita, respondit : 'Ego eram paganus et judex in hoc loco, nec unquam lingua mea protulit iniquam sententiam, quare enim mori non possum donec aqua baptismi renatus ad coelum evolem, quare propter hāc gratiam apud Deum merui.' Baptizato igitur capite, statim lingua in favillam corruit et spiritus ad Dominum evolavit."—*Wernerus Rolevinck Larensis, de Westphalia* (Lib. 1. c. 5).

IT was all in de Stadt Botzen in Tirol, dot der Herr Breitmann shmoked a pipe in a garten under trees mit his friendts a-diskurririn—idly as it war—mit *Abwesenheit* or Absentness of Mind. All at a glance he say :

"Vas it efer to you in a Gallerie befal—dat you all at vonce dink you sees some long forgotted friend or tistant scene; yoost as if you enshanted war—und ven you to yourself *gekommen bist*—you find dot it only a picture is—*ja*—und perhops only a liddle like de vision of your Soul. *Nun*, dis tay as I vas bass de Street along, it mineself come ofer dat I see a friendt dot dis t'irty yar gepuried lies—so drue und reél as couldt pe—*doch* wenn I like again upgewaked bin—id was only an old Gotisch *shteinkop* dot from a stone-carvin' *heraus* stuck. I really dinked it seemed to pe a laughin' at me."

"*Kann sein*," reblied a friend. "Dere ish shtrange dales pout some of dem old headts. Dere is von in Florence—man says dot it was once a real lifin Mönch, vot got into shtone geputrified or *versteinert*, as a punishmendt pecause he maket fun of a griminal dot fore-by goin' to pe beheaded was. Und dot Kopf still py Santa Maria Maggiore to be seen is—fery wondervoll to pehold."

"Und yet dereto," add der Herr Rumpelmeyer, "und more wunderfuller ist de *historia* how in Vienna im Yar Twelf-hundert, a human headt upge-dugged war, dot was all alive—*ja, ganz lebendig.* Und it shpoke de beoples *Lateinisch sehr gut*—in Latin—und ask vot yar it vos, und vanted to know vedder Christianity hot coom along yet? Denn der Episcopus talked it in Latin, und der Kopf say: 'I was a pagan in de Roman dime, und I was *Judex* or Shoodge in dis blace. Und pecause I nefer pronouncet a lie in all mine life, und nefer an unyoost sentence spoked to any man, it was ordainet dat I should not die und go mit de oder Heat'ens, but live till I could pe paptized a Christian.' Denn der *Bischof* baptize dot het— when all at vonce it died und fell into doost— und from it a shpirit rosed oop to Heafen."

"*Ja,* dot is a peautiful shtory," resumet der Rumpelmayer after a short pause mit a long trink of bier—"und yet dere is also a more wunderfoller von of a Student who was geborn in dis fery town of Botzen, dot I in an old manuscript hafe readt. *Und, mit Erlaubniss,* if you bermit, dot tale I vill also norrate pointedly, yoost as it is set doun in a *Chronik* in *Alt-Deutsch* vitch I into modern German over-set will."

Denn he telled dis shtory, vitch I have here into rymes rendered. But id is vort' notice dot dis subject of off-ge-cutted hets is so extentsife dot it a *Buch* py itself deserfes. For dere ist de headt of der physician Douban in the Arabian Nights, mit de headt of Orpheus vot talket to Cyrus, und dot of de priest of Jupiter, und anoder von tescripet by Trallianus, und de marfellously breservet headt of de Saint describet in Olof Tryggvason's Saga, und *De Witch's Headt* of dot crate und genial Mosaic-worker Rider Haggard, mit afer so many more, not to shpeak of de *Teraphim* Kopfs dot were made to shpeak mit tubes—und Friar Bacon's *Caput—ja*, I a Buch write will some tay on dis—*wahrhaftig*. Boot now to de poem.

THE STUDENT AND THE HEAD.

Dere vas vonce a *fahrende* Student,
Dot is a travellin young gent-
Elman—whose regular Cur's it is
To be-seek de tifferent Universities,

Germany—Tyrol.

Und—vot is now pecomin a rarity,
Livin so well as he could from charity,
    Makin his livin
    By oder folks given
Votefer dey hat to shpare *im Noth*,
Som'dimes bennies und som'dimes Brot:

    Alvays gay,
    A-workin his way,
    Gettin along
    Mit shtories und song,
Und rich ven he hat in his bocket a dollar,
Soosh vas de life of Johannes der Scholar.

Nun, gut. Von efenin it comed to bass,
Dot he found himself sittin oopon de grass,
Veary mit walkin, to roost a-while,
Mit nefer a house for many a mile,
Nodings around him but mighdy rocks:
Unt he dinked, "I am now in a fery pad box.
I moost shleep *al fresco*—dere is no dodgin'
De vact—und here I moost make my lodgin':
So he seeket apout, und soon dere vas seen
Vot seemet to pe a liddle *Ruin*
    Of some oldt Tempel,
    A goot *Exempel*
Of py-gone forgotted, heidenisch Races
Dot worshipt in solitudinous blaces,
    Dough really no man
    Couldt say if 'dwas Roman,

Or if, as some offshoot from de Tuscan,
Id hadn't peen bildt py de early Etruscan
Vherein to bractise deir pagan iniquity.
Boot Hans nefer dinked apout dings of antiquity:
He only dinked as a night-sojourner,
Vhere he might find in de ruin a gorner
        To shpread his blanket
           Und afterwarts "spank it,"
Py broke of tay from where he'd peen restin',
Vitch was not to him in de least interestin'.
Denn he pulled out a bread mit a biece of *Wurst*
Und a flask of Riesling to conquer his Durst,
        Vitch 'twas difficult work
        At foorst to un-cork,
So it comed to bass dot some trops of der Wein
Py de merestest accident fell on a Stein,
Und vot vas der Student's awe mit dread,
Ven he heard a Voice dot solemly said:

    "Is't an offering from dee,
      Stranger vitch dou pringest me?
      Tausend yars have bassed away,
      Since I here neglected lay,
      All forgotten und alone,
      Here peneat' dis altar-shtone,
      Und vot is de fery worst,
      Mit neer a trop to squinch my *Durst;*
      Und du bist der Erst, allein,
      Who has efer gived me Wein;

Germany—Tyrol.

    Boot if dou would'st gaze on me,
    Lift dis shtone und you will see
    Somedings dot will you soorprize,
    Right pefore your fery eyes."

Johannes was druly not wantin in boldness,
Boot dis dings shivert him foorst mit coldness,
Yed shakin it off to himself he say,
" I will see dis troo, let dere come vot may!"
Und so mit a heave und denn mit a groan,
He finally liftet dot altar-shtone.
For 'twas derriply hard inteed to raise it,
Und ven 'twas done he was sore amazet!
For the sight he peheld was py no means a common
    'un,
Boot a fery unusuallest phenomenon,
For all in a cup of porphyry red,
Dere lay pefore him a human head!

Von instant he gazed in silence unproken,
Denn dinkin on vot de Voice had shpoken,
Mit fery gommendaple presence of mine,
He poured in de mout' of de het some wine;
Ven 't smocked its lipps—as vas perfegdly blain—
Exglaimin' mit tignity, " Do it again!"
Und der het took it in, dough it hadn't a t'rottle,
Oontil it exoctly half finish't de pottle,
Denn greatly refreshet—venn dis vas done—
Open't its talker und dus pegun:

"Ere de fery earliest hisdory dime,
Ven die Werlt und soosh dings were in deir prime,
I was priest und a leader in dis lan',
Und gen'rally reckoned an hon'raple Mann;
Liddle py liddle I rosed in learnin',
Liddle py liddle great dings discernin',
Liddle py liddle to higher station,
Dill at last I had a refelation
Dat when I a tausent goot deets had done,
My worldly career its corse would hafe run,
Und free from mortal droples und strife
I shouldt rise to de higher and heafenly life.

"Yet dere was a *magus* who hated me
Mit de spite of a *Teufel*, right pitterly,
Who had me slain ere mine course vas run,
Und only de half of my dask vas tone;
Vitch, as sure ash de Sonn' opon mordals shines,
Vas *lignea dura*—fery hardt lines!
Yet a Higher Power comed und said:
Dot I shouldt not die, aldough I vas deadt,
For mein het, dot my murd'rer had off ge-cut,
Shouldt into dis fery shrine pe put,
Und py goot atfice to beoples in needs,
Shouldt work oud de rest of my excellend deeds.

"Und so it went as dis Power ordain't,
Dill only von hundert to do remain't.
Ven lo! dis enemy of mine
Set de Romans on to our shrine,

Germany—Tyrol.

Vitch dose who were drue to our fait' und me,
Closed oop and ruined as here you see,
Flyin' away in sorrow mit tears,
Und left me—von hundert still—in arrears.
So now all hope is goned afay,
Und I most lie here till de Yungest Tay :
Dot is to say, dill a tay of Doom,
Mit my soul a livin' in dis Tomb.
Nun, gut. You hafe gived me an instand's bleasure,
Und I dells you somedings—dere is a Treasure
A lyin' peneat' dis fery shtone,
Und I gife it unto you, all for your own;
You gave me wein for vitch I did yearn,
So now I'll do somedings for you in turn."

Now dis our Johannes—*omnibus*—
By all was called *bonus socius*
Or a right goot veller, und generous Mann,
Vot Deutschers term *ein wackrer Kumpàn*,
Und in von ding he laid all de rest on de shelf,
Py dinkin of oders pefore himself,
Vitch of all dings in all humanity,
Amounts to de doppermost Christianity :
So de instand de *Kopf* dese worts hat spottet,
He holler mit yoy " *Donnerwetter*—I've got it !
You may pet your het on a rapid escape,
Und dot I will get you out of dis scrape,
Und in twendy-four hours mitout denyin'
Your soul will oop into Heafen go vlying :
Like a kite or a pird mit vings,

Und dis is de way to manage de dings:
Dot treasure vot you hafe given to me,
In a hundert parts shall divitet pe,
Und afery share mitout any bodder,
I'll gife to some poor devil or odder,
Und as sure ash in rifers you'll find some reeds,
Dot'll shoost make oop your hundert goot teeds,
Denn like an arrow you'll scoot afay,
Isn't it yolly! Hip—hoo—*hooray!*"

A shmile sdole ofer de face sedate
Of de het dot lay in de porph'ry blate,
Unt dus to Johannes it did say:
" Dou art formed I ween of de finest clay
Dot men are made of." To put it "quick,"
It meant to say that Hans vas a brick,
Und ve most admit, regardin dis yout'
Dot der Head vasn't fery far off from de trut'.
But it only remarkt: " Pray dake de treasure,
Und go und pestow it avay at your bleasure,
As dou hast saidt, among de boor,
Und denn, return to dis blace vonce more."

Hans liftet der shtone as he'd peen told,
Und foundt von hundert bieces of gold,
Und to cut it short, der fery next tay,
Vent trav'lin' apout on de sharity lay,
Und founded de trut' of de sayin' dot givin'
Is forty dimes petterer foon dan receive 'n.

Germany—Tyrol.

Dere's noding so schweet vile on eart' we live—
Dot is to say *when we've got it to give*—
Got it to give—und dink we can spare it—
Dere is de point on which turns de merit
Of cuttin' out slices—you might call dem frustrumers—
Nun—Hans knew de roadts und hat plenty of customers,
Und vit'in a tay all de cash hat gone vlyin'—
So happy und gay he return'd to de shrine.

De curtain of tarkness had gaddered o'er
De *Bett* of Night ash he com'd to de toor,
When lo! pefore his 'stonish't sight
Dere stoot a wondrous Vision of light:
Vitch seemet oonto his shtartled mind
De fairy-est sort of de angel kind,
Or else, *per contra*, to poot id square, he
Might call it de most angelic-al fairy;
Anyhow doun on his knees he fell,
Und said "Now I see id has all gone well!"

"Yea," say de Vision, "Danks to dee,
All has inteed gone well mit me;
For de insdant de last of dem coins was spent,
Up to de sky in dis form I went,
Und now I redurn boot for vonce, mine Sohn,
To dank dee for all of de goot dou hast tone."
"*Gratias tibi*," quot' Hans, "Dough you've saidt it,
I really ton't dink I teserfe any credit

Hans Breitmann in Germany—Tyrol.

For roonin apout und cuttin' a dash,
Und doin' of goot oopon oder folk's cash;
Most beople wouldt find it exdremely funny
Helpin' de boor—if you'd find dem de money:
Now if de money hat peen mine own,
I'd have shpent it all oopon you alone,
I shvears I vouldt done it—yoost de same—
Und denn I'd have hat som' sort of a claim;
Boot as id is, I only, sure,
Hafe had a goot dime—relievin' de boor!"

De Spirit smilin' replied, "I see,
Boot if *dot* is dy idea of a spree,
Vitch might de hardest Temperance soften,
It's a bity you cannot go on 'em more often.
If dis is de vay you always act,
I dells you Johannes—und it is a fact—
If on soosh dissipation you ofden go it,
You'll get to Heafen before you know it;
Toornet to an Angel, und dot is drue,
Dot is vot happens to rowdies like you:
Nun gut, mein Sohn—peneat' yon shtone,
Lies a pigger *Schatz* dan de previous von.
Take it und puy dee a county and castle,
Dere is de specie—go do up de parcel."

Johannes follet de angel's word,
Und grew'd to pe an opulent Lord.
Dis Story teaches itself its lesson,
So needs no moral. Denn dake my plessin!

CHAPTER VIII.

ON TYROLESE FIG-COFFEE UND DE SOCIOLOGICAL DEDUCTIONS FROM IT. MIT A BALLADE APOUT DIS DING OF CHEMICAL METAGENESES UND MYSDERIÖS METASTASES.

" Dass einst die Chemie im Bunde mit den anderen Naturwissenschaften alle möglichen Nahrungsmittel kunstlich herstellen werde."—WERNER VON SIEMENS.

Go vhere you may in a Tiroler toun—und esbecially in Innsbruck — you will berceife shdealin over de air a *Schmell* vitch, in dime, unto you so Tyrolean pecomes dot yoost ash *Bier* und ratishes do Munich recal—or violets Florence—so dis odour or anydnig like it pring to mind a handbill vitch eferywhere to be seen is—mit a bicture of a ferocious *Gamsjäger* or chamois hunter, und die Worts, *Accht Tyroler Feigen-Kaffé*, or "Genuine Tyrolese Fig-Coffee."

De aroma in question vitch is somedings like de *bouquet de brown sugar* burning mit toast—from de *Fabrik* or factories proceeds vhere dis Aid to de Afflicted in Purse is made. In tashte it is, as der Americaner said, "Not excisely nice nor prezactly nasty"—und he who it has hat de misfordune to trink, will (if he knows dem), find it not so nasty, nor poisonous to de liver nor injurious to de nerves as chicory—in fact no petter nor vorse dan de *café* dot is made of acorns, or rye or wheat, or sweet-potatoes—or ground nuts—or peas, or peans or burnt maize grits—or most of such peverages as pecame familiar unto our soldiers—as well as to de First Families of de Sout'—during de American Civil War. To my own balate de *Chicory-café*—as dispenset at all de first-class hotels in Germany —peginnin' wit the fery first in Cologne—is py far de most unpleasantest in daste, as it is for healt' de worst—as is seen py too many sallow shildren and girls who are specially poisoned mit it.

Germany—Tyrol.

De fig-caffé is howefer mate indo a paste witch into imitation coffee seeds or peans[1] is fabricated witch looks brecisely like real *caffè*—a process witch is quite *überflüssig*, as Ficks do not look like any soosh dings—oonless de object pe to sooply schwindlin' small grocers mit somedings to bass off for real *café*—which dey indeed do—all ofer Europe on de poor—danks to Tyroler enderprize und infentiveness! Of all which crate enterprizers und infentors—whedder dey pe known ash Promoters, Speculators, Syndicators, Floaters, Trusters, Stock-Investors for de Ignorant, Money Lenders mit no Fees Required, Sand und Sugar Mixers or Coffee-bean imitators—I can only reëcho de prief yudgement of Herr Breitmann—" *Tamn de whole lot!* "

Vhen he saidt dis memoraple ding, it was in

[1] *Café Beans—Bohnen.*—Der Herr George Augustus Sala in dot inderestin Buch of his: "Dings I hafe seened und Beoples I hafe knowed," fery broperly remarks dot " That which is erroneously known as a bean is in reality the *seed* of a berry " (vol. ii. p. 59). Und he is quite right. But der is also an error in callin' cherry und peach-seeds shtones, und I am not morally sure apout orange-pips.

Hans Breitmann in

a *café* where man had really servet him mit goot *Mocha*—und id vas his amazement und telight at findin' such a ding in a land where German gespoken was, dot led to dese casual remarks on Fig-Coffee. Py him sat der Herr Schwefelbrenner, a tistinguished *Chemicus*—und he, after a bause opservet:

"Dot is all fery drue—Shickory is a poison und Fick Café is nashty, boot dou shouldst rememper dot dere moost a peginnin' pe to all dings—und py and py, *die Chemie* de fery aroma und perfection of coffee will gife, very sheap. Meandimes——"

"Ja," remark der Student, "but it is dot *ad interim* vitch is doin' more harm dan all your infentions are wort. I asked a *Kellner* in a crate hotel vy dey poot shickory indo de café. ' *Vot !* ' he esglaim, ' Don't you like it ? *All* our guesds like a *liddle*,—yoost to improfe de flavour. Most beoples prefer it, Sir.' I ashk a cook in dis town 'pout fick *café*. 'Vell,' he say, "We poot *yoost a liddle* in to gife a fine colour und pody to de *café*—beoples *like* to see dot.' Now dis is all simbly mean *schwindlin*. If a man pays you goot money in full, and ashks for butter or *café* you hafe no right to sell him Oléomargarine or fick-paste, no matter how goot it is. If you do, you are a low *scamp*—a *Hallunke*—und noding else. Und dot wort, ' yoost a *liddle*—to improve it,' always cofers a *lie*—it mean fifty *per cent*. Now we are alfays hearin' gomplaints of de exclusifeness of Society, and how beople is look't doun oopon pecause of deir callin's. *Nun, gut*—vhen de retailin' class in all de valks of life shtop sellin' ficks und shickory for *café* und lyin' apout it—denn de greatest parrier to equality will pe remofed—argue de point ash man will. Goot Society—howefer padly it succeeds—means Honour und Dignity—or it *tries* to."

"Truly I admit all dot," rebly der Brofessor, "but I dink you should not gonfound de mere rascals who perfert *Chemie*, mit men of Science. Vot I say is, dot ere long Science will gife to Man wholesom' und acreeaple food, *ad libitum*, fery sheap, so dot an immense amount of sufferin' moost pecome reliefed. Dus we can alreaty make Oleomargarine, vitch is truly *bona-fide* butter—

und only has a pad name, pecause a crate deal
—berhaps most of it—is made py rascals who
manufacture it from vile trash—sheaply. Und
aprobos of dis, Meine Herren—it is fery curios
dot der vas, efen in de most anciendt dimes, an
Idee dot Butter couldt—esbecially by Witches
—pe maked out of gommon, *sogar* nashty dings.
Dus in a *Buch*, named *Der Glückstopf* py
Johannes Praetorious of 1669, I foundt dis
sayin'—
>'Kühedreck und Butter
>Kömbt von einer Mutter.'

Und chemically dot is someding like true.
Und die Perfumers hafe peen accuset mit some
inyustis of usin' dis inderesdin' soopstance (vitch
is inteed holy and sacred in India), to make
schweet fragrances mit—und no ashtonishing-
ness do I derein find vhen I dinks dot Man
gets tree telicious aromas from coal alone—mit
a *bouquet* dat schmell so goot ash nefer vas—*ja*
—und if you will rememper dot in 1851 dere was
exhibit at de World's Fair in London four
pottles of goot shpirits made from der *shmoke*
of a factory shimney, you may add to dese de

Germany—Tyrol.

otto of whiskey dot der Englander Thackeray mention. *Ach du Lieber Gott!*"—he added mit enthusiasm—"Vhen I dinks of de Hydro-carbons denn I veel mine soul schwim in holy fisions of de future, und my réligiöse Gefühl exbress itself in my

"CREDO."

"Dis is de true und only Creed
In vitch I do pelieve indeed;
All dings, as de Chemie dells,
Can pe made of Someding Else.
As Lime is made of Oyster Shells,
Und bottles oft are turned to bells
Und shtinkin dings to lofely shmells,
So from bitumen, at command,
We kit de shweet *paté d'amande*,
Also anoder vitch dey say
Is somedings like de Ess Bouquet.
Und out of Coal as may pe seen
Wax cantles—dot is paroffine,
An oil dere mit vitch pring de dollars
Und many kinds of lofely colours;
I cannot dell oopon my soul
Vot 'dis you cannot make from coal.
Und also Bread as com' it must
From wood ven sawed—dot is de dust,
So dot in efery trunk ve'll see
In dime to com' a bread-fruit dree.

> From wood we mak' too—dot is queer
> Ash I hafe seen, de best *Papier*,
> Und cider oft abbears again
> Upon our daple as champagne;
> Und so 'twill pe ven we are gone
> Dis shange of soobject vill go on,
> Und tifferent kinds of tifferent dings
> From tifferent sorts of objects shbrings,
> Oontil . . . .

—*Ja*—dot is enough of dot—de soopyect of Transformations is capabel of moosh commentation."

"*Das ist wahr*," reblied der Student. "Und I know a fery *curiose ballade* of an oldt shtory dot illusdratet it foorst rate."

Und mitout vaitin' to pe asket, opservin' a shmile in de affirmative in all de circum-surrounding countenances, he dook oop de guitar, und mit an *arpeggio* began as follows:—

DER ALTE TAPPEINER.

Vherefer in dis worldt we go,
Dere's farious fancies as we know.
Soom dake a pride in wicketness,
Soom trow demselfs afay on tress,

Germany—Tyrol.

Ja, growed-oop men oft show deir follies
In tressing oop deir liddle Dollies—
Py vitch we blainly see oh friendt
Dot all are shildren in de *Endt*.

      But of all trash,
      To say de least,
      Is to sbend all your cash
      On your weddin' feast ;
To trow avery cent on your friendts avay,
Und hafe nodding to eat on de vollerin tay :—
      Vitch still to de present,
      Fool many a peasant
In de Tirol continues to do,
Und vile a shtarvin' he'll say to you :
"You dink I am boor, and it truly may pe,
Boot nopody hat a *weddin'* like me ;
Und it shtill is de talk of all in de shpot,
I shpent all I hat in de vorlt, py Gott !
Dere's noding like goin' it ven you try,
Und I wasn't wed in a gorner—not I."
So de Irish peasants in Donegal
Shpend all a man leaves on his funeral ;
Und to make for a day a show—observe—
On de next dey leave his shildren to starve ;
      So in de Tyrol,
      I peliefe on my soul,
If a girl must choose ; not hafin de room ;
She'd prefer de wedding unto de groom :
For you can find fellers as pees find honey,

Hans Breitmann in

In avery field, ven de vedder is sunny,
But to hafe a swell weddin' costs lashins of money,
De whole of it meanin'—as vell we know
De mainspring of vulgar minds is—Show!
Videlicet—monstrari digito,
To pe *dalked apout*—no matter py whom,
To pe *pointed at* in avery room,
To pe *stared at* in any company,
No matter how low de starers may pe.
Und oh vot ropturous etereal vapour
Dey breat'e at seein' deir names in de paper!
E'en if dey sended dem in demself,
No matter—dey're *dere*—on de public shelf!
Mit dieves und American millionaires,
Bolice reports und all fancy wares,
Und similar trash with noding in't,
No matter—deir names are dere, *in print!*

 Nun, in Tyrol dere is a blace
 Of vitch a proferb say mit grace,
  Dot " *Pinet, Lechtl und Tappein*
  Sein die drei schönsten Hof, die im Landl sein,"
Or dot "Pinet, Lechtl, Tappein—at command—
Are de tree finest blaces in all de Land."
Tappein of dem is de best' position,
Und in it vonce lifed an olt Magician
Who could do all kind of wunderfoll dings
Whose memorie shtill troo de country rings:
Item. He couldt toorn dust into salt,
Item. De vorst of dirt into malt,

Germany—Tyrol.

Item. Screws into goot horses to suit ye
Item—an ugly girl to a peauty ;
Item. Afder a short diagnosis
He'd work any kind of a metamorphosis
Ash Italian artists by avocation
Toorn any old Daub to a Transfiguration,
Und a Pintorello to what dey sell
For a shplendid, undoubted Raphaèl.
Nun, gut—in dese dings der old scamp was a shiner
Und beople call'd him *Der alte Tappeiner.*

    Near py, dere lifed a lofely maiden,
    Who mit sorrow was oberladen ;
    A girl who was proud as she was poor ;
    No fery uncommon ding to pe sure ;
Und de gause of her drople was dis, d'ye see,
Dot she ere long ge-married moost pe
To a man whom she lofed. 'Twas *curios*,
Yet nod afder all soosh a sinkular case.
Und de gause of her crief may all pe said in
Few worts—dat she couldn't afford a fine weddin'
Mit a regular swell und elegant feast,
Vhere efery man could get trunk ash a peast,
On wine of the pest—de whole py night
To endt in a *Rauferei*, or fight
Mit *Stossrings*, vists und lecks of chairs ;
Denn 'twould pe heardt—und averywheres—
"'Tvas de vinest Weddin' dot efer I saw,
Mit all dot we wanted—und more—*gelt ja !* "

Nun—von night as she sat
Like a woe-begone cat
Full of de dismals, horrors und doomps,
Vorse dan a plue teufel down mit de moomps
Or a Pessimist in de Slough of Despond,
Or any soosh sorryfool vacapond,
Lookin' altogeder as if she were mighty
Far gone in low spirits und *tædium vitæ*,
In a wild strange blace py de light of de moon
Vhere a torrent roared in a monotune
Py a dark cafern openin' dere,
Dot von might have schwored was de Cave of Tespair,
Ash she heafed a sigh in de mournfollest mood,
Der alte Tappeiner pefore her shtood.

Mit movin' force "Mein shild" saidt he,
" I know de cause of dy misery,
Und if I moost druly the truth confess
Dou has fery goot reason for wretchedness :
For de beoples is all peginnin' to say,
Dot if you e'er com' to a weddin' tay,
Id will pe de *meanest*—upon my soul !
Dot efer was seen in der Land Tirol,
De shappiest und most poferdy-strucken,
De cheapest und mostest Gott-forsucken,
Und dot in all dime forefer on
Id will pe ash De Peggar's Weddin' known.
Und all at your name will laugh und hiss,
Ja nodin couldt pe so tiscraceful as dis ;

Germany—Tyrol.

Und id vills my soul mit sympatie,
For dis I am coomed to weep mit dee!"

    Now vhen he hat said
    Dese Worts, de Maid—
Her name was Pauline—hat a crate sensation
Of rage mit horror und admiration,
All in a serial concatenation,
Rage at de *Comperendination,*
Dot is "delay"—of de nuptialization,
Horror at de recapitulation
Of all dot caused her desperation,
Mingled mit fery crate opprobation
Of de fery exact exemplification
Of all dot caused her humiliation;
Aldough it hurt worse dan scarification,
Or tearin' de flesh py excarnification—
Nun, gut—she was prought to a peaudiful shtate,
Ash der wizard wanted—of shame und hate,
Und to raise de wind for her marriage-revel,
Reaty to go mit herself to de tevil.

Und denn mit a foice dot was kind und sad:
He saidt, "It may pe dot dings are not so pad;
From all kints of drople dere's some esgape,
Und alvays a way out of avery scrape;
Und if you had only courage and spirit
De fence a'nt so high but vot you may clear it;
But dot is de quesdion—*hafe* you de courage?"
Now dis Pauline for a maiden of *her* age,

As all dot knowed her did soon atmit,
Was fery well off for sand und grit,
Vitch mak's friendts und foes—since remarkaply odd
   it is
We admire vhile we fear dese sterling commodities,
So mit a grim shmile she answered " You
Hat petter dell me vot I moost do :
Tune oop your fiddle, und oben de Ball,
I dinks I can tanz'—if courage is all."

Der alte Tappeiner regart de maid
Mit admiradion und denn he said :
" Dis worlt ist all gomposet of lies,
In farious colours of avery size,
  Lies apout men,
  Und lies apout women ;
  Und Lies acain
  Apout Averyding human,
Lies apout Poferty, lies apout Riches,
Lies apout womens a vearin de preeches,
Lies apout avery Somepody vitch is
Petter ash oders—especially Witches,
Who are really, of all, de fery pest,
Und py far de most misrepresentedest ;
For dough 'tis not generally oondershtood
Dey basses deir dime in doin' good."
(*Sotto voce*, " good to demselfs.")
" Und ash for de shtories of Teufels und Elfs
Dey are mosdly inshpir'd py noding but malice,
Und all moost pe daken *cum grano salis*.

Germany—Tyrol.

Und in our eyes dere so moosh dust is
Regardin' all dis, dot to do dem yoostis,
Shpeakin' of dem de actual verity,
Dey are oonly a kind of Sisders of Sharity,
Mit penevolent aims of vitch de result is
Dey lofe to help beople in tifficùlties,
Und most of all to assisdt a maiden
Who vants a stylish und handsome veddin';
Deir brinciples—dake 'em for all in all,
Are de Communistic Idéal,
Omnium-gatherum Liberàl,
Mixtum-compositum Sociàl,
Nefer a-droplin' demselfs mit diforces,
Flyin' apout on prooms for horses,
Leadin' soosh peaudiful practical lives
Dey've no dime to dink apout hoospans or wifes;
Sailin' so fast dey forget de cargo,
Moosh ash de beople life in Chicago:
Vitch of all blaces peneat' de sun
Is a Witches' Nest—if dere efer vas von.
Now if you vish to hoppy pe,
You hat petter yoin de Society,
Und denn my tear you will hafe, I ween,
Soosh a woonderful Weddin' ash nefer was seen."

Paulina lisden't to afery wort,
Und schwallow it doun—but de half she heardt
Was enof to convert her—ash von may say
She met der Tappeiner more dan half way;

So dey make't a trade, und de fery first ding
He promist to make her a gay wed-díng,
Mit soosh a drementous und shplendid feast
Ash nefer vas seen from West to East
Or from Nort' to Sout'—or from Pole to Pole
Or anywhere else in *ganz* Tirol.

  Den at de last
  Dere came de weddin',
   Ven dime was past
  Und the guests were bidden ;
Fünf hundert beople—none left pehind—
Hungry ash wolfs dot's peen livin' on wind ;
For devourin' and scowrin'—all of von mind,
Soosh as at rural tinners you find.
Und 'twas berfectly blain ven you look at der taple
Der wizard had done vot art was aple,
Knowin' fery well vot fisch und flesh meant
In afery form for human refreshment,
Und noding dot could e'er be missed
Py de sarco-ichthyophagist.
  Everyding for nutriment,
  Dot Natur in Tyrol has sent,
  Dainties, victuals ediple
  In quantity incrediple ;
  Meat mit prog comestible,
  Und afery dings digestible,
  First de *hors d'oeuvres* dot coom from France
  Mit many a *pièce de resistance*,

Germany—Tyrol.

Peaches in preserve mit quinces,
Fricasses, ragouts und minces,
Broth und *Suppé*, spoon-meat, pasty,
Caviar—vot some dinks nasty—
Puddins, bies mit omelette,
Anchovies de taste to whet,
Lofely custards at your winkin',
Butterbrod mit beef und Schinken;
Averyding in de way of Victuals,
Toornin spits und shteamin kittles—
—Oxens roasted whole mit Schwein—
Und—donnerwetter!—ach der Wein!
Parrels of Wein, und Wein in pottles,
Wein from der Rhein for dusty t'rottles,
Flasks vot look like long processions
Of holy monks a-gifin blessin's!
For dey seem like priests dot are long robes
    dres't in,
Und dese to der crowd were most interestin'!

Nun—dey coom to der feast, boot yoost ash de Lady,
Or Bride, was a goin' to say, "'Tis ready!"
    She grew pale mit awe
    At Somedings she saw,
Among dose who were ready to pegin,
Und dat was a reverend Capuchin.
    Ja wohl, she was faint
    At de sight of dot saint,
Und she couldn't move an arm or a leg—oh!
Vhen he say, "*Tibi Deo, gratias ago!*"

Hans Breitmann in

      Gott vot a sight
      Of awe and affright
Vas peheld py all de derrified crowd
Ash dey ootered a shkreem remarkably loud !
Und dey all ash Deutschers say were Spanished [1]
Vhen right pefore dem de whole feast vanish't.

      Dey shtare und dey look ;
      Ja—it all was a *Spuk !*
Glamour und humpug und idle Shine,
'Twas out mit de Vittles und out mit der Wein,
Out mit de hope of a gay carouse,
Und a regular case of *Nix komm' heraus.*
      Down in der room
      In a swoon fell de Groom,
Vhile Paulina went whirrin' away on her broom!

Now vhen dey com' to examine de Feast,
'Twas a nasty show for to say de least,
Und man wouldt hafe said dot sight to see,
Id was yoost de stoff vitch moderne *Chemie*
Mit de aid of retorts, und acids und kittles,
Vould toorn, if it could, into peaudifool vittles.

[1] *Das kommt mir Spanisch vor.* "*So wird von einer Sache gesagt die befremdet, unangenehm, wohl auch komisch wirkt.* Dat looks Spanish to me is said of any ding dot is strange disagreeable und queer." So say der Borchhardt in his Buch on German Proferbs. Der Goethe use dis exbression in his Egmont (III. 2).—" Ich versprach dir, einmal Spanisch zu kommen."

Germany—Tyrol.

Und fery poor food to marry on,
For de meat vas all horriple carrion—
Or *Aas*—dot is, of ass und horse,
Vitch is rader poor food for a regular course,
Dough the Paris Hippophage Society
Dink it is nice py way of variety ;
De apples too were only *fæces*,
Dat is of de fery peculiar species,
Dat oncet remark't, " Pehold how we shwim,"
Und nefer fell from no opple-drees' lim' ;
  Vhile as for de drink
  Ach !—dere I must shrink
From gifin a gloser tetailed analysis,
It wasn't de sort dot you meets mit in palaces ;
For dough it was druly an Ur-Rhein Wein,
Or ancient, I cannot tescripe it as *fein*,
No more mine page mit soosh dings to muddle :
'Twas vintage out of some fery old puddle ;
All had peen made in der Teufel's kitchen ;
To rival vitch is der Chemist's ambition ;
De cookin' of vitch in Macbéth we read—
Nun, gut—Gluck zu ! Led oos hope he'll succeed !

" Dot Ballade," remark der Herr Breitmann, " *hat eine geniale Anwendung*—a glefer opplication to vot earlier remarket has peen on technical Chemistry. Therefore I dank dis yung shendleman for it."

"*Was des Teufel's Küche betrifft*—concerning der Teufel's Kitchen," say der Student, who appeared to pe a *feiner* Herr—"in der mittel age vhen Witches mit der Teufel carried on deir *infame* liddle games of sorcery, dot was called der Teufel's, or die Witches' Kitchen, vhence come der proverb *In des Teufel's Küche kommen*, to get into der defil's kitchen, dot mean to get into drople. Somedimes it was ge-called de Black Kitchen, und der Goethe uses it in dot sense, vhere der Faust say :

"'Mein Father vas a toubtful honest man
Who in de gompany of de Adepti,
In der *Black Kitchen* shoot himselfs away,
Und afder recipes innumeraple
Poured indo von vot is most gontrary.'"[1]

"*Nun gut*," say der Breitmann, "may we all pe proud of it—*und trink ! Vivat Sequenz !*"

"*Sequenz*," remark der Herr Doctor who hat

[1] *Faust* I. 686. Dis is from der Herr Breitmann his dranslation of Faust dot will pooplisht pe ven von hundert tausend *Abonnenten* or supscripers deir names to der Herr T. Fischer Unwin, in-senden will, mit an autograps of de author on der vlyleaf.

yoost come in, " ist to remark dot I drust dot our friendt der Herr Breitmann will recordt soom of his *Imbressions te Foyage* in der Tyrol in a Buch."

"*Kann sein*," moormur der Breitmann, "Boot venn a veller hat soosh *Idees* he petter keep his *silentium*, for ash de sayin' is,

   " ' Wer reisen will
    Der schweige still ! '

Or—

   " Der drafeller's law
    Is ' Holt your jaw ! ' "

" *Wohl*," reblied der Brofessor, " It coom indo mine het dot vonce on a dimes der shendleman whose name we know from its pein associated on de ditle-pages mit dot of our friendt Breitmann, broposet when he was goin' to shbend some mont's in Amerika to wride some letters to a London Refiew. Oopon vitch der Editor remark dot dose Letters would read a goot deal like ' Dravels amoong de Cannibals py von of deir Shiefs.'[1] Und dot is vot id seems to me

[1] Dis moost pe, *ohne Zweifel*, der Herr—*sit verbo venia !*—regartin whom I would remark dot if any of de readers hafe any bleasure found in de Legends

dot der Herr Breitmann is among dese Tyrolers —almost too moosh of der same colour to pe distinguishet. Howefer as a broof of de eatin' is in de poodin, we shall know more pout dot vhen we com' to see his *Buch*."

"*Das hängt davon ab*," reply der Breitmann, "Dot depends not on de soopyect more dan on *das Gemüth* or de humour, or feelin', or sympatic of der autor's mind. *Die wunderschöne Frau*, Madame Linda Villari—whose Englisch is ash sweet und lovely as her face — bemerks mit artist's percepdion in her Italian Sketches how fresh und vigorous und shtrong de Tyrolese moundain-land seem compared mit dot of Italy. *Nun*—vhere a man has a land like *dot* to deal mit, der pestest ding he can do is to yoost set town vot he sees, afder his own *Gemüth* mitout takin' or makin' hard work, vitch is not vot a crate manys do. Let das Land yoost mirror itself in your mind——"

und Shtories in dis *Buch*, dey will not less interested pe in his Work on de Legends of Florence as told py de People (now in bress py D. NUTT, 270, Strand, London).

Germany—Tyrol.

"*Ja*—" add der Student mit a smile, "but let de *frame* of de mirror pe all your own design, so moosh as bossiple. *Trink aus!*—und luck to you!

> "Praecor omnia læta vobis omnibus,
> Deus bene fortunet vestrum convivium!"
>
> (I pray you all may yolly pe!
> Gott pless de daple und companie!)

SCHLUSSWORT.

Go fort' mein Büchlein out of hand!
'Twill com' to pass I ween,
A copie 'll go into som' Land
Vhere I hafe nefer peen;
Und vhen I dink oopon dot case,
Id seem so strange to me;
My t'oughts can go indo a blace
Vhere I can nefer pe!

Dot is der Writer's sveetest Tream,
Vitch he can ne'er forget,
Dot he may cast von sunny gleam
On those he ne'er has met;
Und he who's luck to work dis spell,
Dis sweetest Sorcerie—
Has shown dot he has mastered well,
Life's wunderbar'st Magie.

Hans Breitmann in Germany—Tyrol.

Farewell *mein Buch*—*adje* mein Friendt !
We two may nefer meet,
We'fe come togeder to de Endt
Un yed, tid nefer meet !
Dot seems an contradict'ry sense,
I hope dot it vill pe
De only point of tifference
Vat coom 'twix you and me.

———

" I, Liber ac orbi docto te publicus infer ! "

www.ingramcontent.com/pod-product-compliance
Lightning Source LLC
Chambersburg PA
CBHW020308170426
43202CB00008B/542